ENDO

George Cromwell's expressive publication, *Flames of Fire*, embers the heart of every preacher and pastor. Cromwell places on paper the true essence of every individual who has a moment of reflection in the very presence of God. It is through these significant chapters you will be able to find the "true" presence and essence of God on printed pages.

This writing is designed to assist the church to come out of hibernation and live out its true purpose (*imago dei*, the image of God) in our contemporary society. Cromwell captures the glimpse of God and the reflection of human personality. Oftentimes, it is difficult to see God in the presence and life of the believer, however, Cromwell does with words what a photographer does with a camera. The image is captured in that moment and leaves an indelible imprint that is timeless. *Flames of Fire* is a must read for each and every believer.

—**Paul L. Anderson,** Pastor
Baptist Grove Church, Inc.
Raleigh, North Carolina

This book is a must for the Christian who is interested in spiritual growth. It is both scholarly and practical. Rev. George Cromwell has done an outstanding job with a subject that touches on spiritual warfare and enters the arena of the full gospel teaching that is a must for growing saints.

Rev. Cromwell is a prolific writer and an outstanding minister of the gospel. This book will eventually become a classic and bless the church.

—**C. E. Willie,** III, Pastor
Rush Metropolitan AME Zion Church
Raleigh, North Carolina

It gives me great pleasure to endorse this book written by Rev. George Cromwell, a former classmate at Southeastern Baptist Theological Seminary of Wake Forest, NC. This book, *Flames of Fire*, is full of inspiration as it deals with the driving force behind God-called preachers, the Spirit of God. In order for us to be effective as pastors and preachers of the gospel, we must burn with Holy Ghost Fire.

—Rev. **Dr. George Jones**
Faith Missionary Baptist Church
Raleigh, North Carolina

FLAMES
OF
FIRE

JOIN THE QUEST FOR BECOMING A FLAME OF FIRE FOR GOD

GEORGE CROMWELL

WinePressPublishing
Great Books, Defined.

ISBN 13: 978-1-60615-040-5
ISBN 10: 1-60615-040-5
Library of Congress Catalog Card Number: 2010921259

DEDICATION

To the Holy Trinity for the inspiration and endurance needed to write *Flames of Fire*.

To the two greatest women who ever undertook to rear a child: my dear mother, Anna Jane Cromwell, a great lady, and to my dear sister, Anna Louise Thomas, whose assistance insured my successful rearing. I shall forever be grateful to these grand and wonderful ladies.

To my wife, Gail L. Cromwell, an inspiration in my walk with God.

To the Rev. Claude E. Willie, III, a great friend, whose encouragement and support are unconditional and continuous.

CONTENTS

ACKNOWLEDGMENTS

I wish to thank Treka Spraggins, a great friend and first typist of this work. Over the years of my writing this manuscript, she became my adopted sister. Then, I acknowledge, with tremendous appreciation, Eula Turner, who had the godly audacity to edit and type this work for publication.

FOREWORD

It is with humility and pleasure that I share some personal thoughts on George T. Cromwell, Sr.'s book, *Flames of Fire*. This book is tremendous light from heaven to many individuals who feel that the church was birthed for more than they have experienced. It is an honest and well-documented account of the life of Abraham and his obedience to God.

Abraham's life of obedience and faith is a testament of the rewards of enduring to the end and blessings will overtake you. Cromwell is presenting a ministerial model for God's ministers. They are seeking insightful revelation and impartation that will revive them and cause their hearts to burn again.

I compare this feeling of hearts burning again with Cleopas' discussion with those who were with him and encountered Jesus following His resurrection. It is written: "And they said one to another, 'Did not our heart burn within us, while he talked with us by the way, and while he opened to us the scriptures?'" (Luke 24:32).

Over the years the professional clergy has managed to water down what was started in the Old Testament as well as that which was birthed in Jerusalem known as the first century church.

Cromwell's book will move you from the coldness entrenched in tradition to a flaming fire for God.

Flames of Fire has been written for God's chosen servants who refuse to be ordinary and who are bold enough in *Him* to do extraordinary works! This work will impact the kingdom of God as it brings glory and honor to the King of kings.

—**Bishop L. Foday Farrar,** Pastor
Solid Rock Ministry International
Garner, North Carolina

INTRODUCTION

To yield to the call of God not knowing exactly where He is leading—like Abraham, who was called from his father's house and kindred to seek the promised land of success in the Lord—is one of the greatest acts of faith a person ever undertakes. The call of God may be a vision or the inner knowing in the heart that surely God and only God has called one to minister the glorious gospel of Jesus Christ. This same gospel is the power of God unto salvation for all people of every nation, creed, and race. This is the same gospel that contains the words of redemption to Christ and forgiveness of sins, provision for daily living, healing for the physically sick, as well as mending of the heart to those whose spirits have been crushed.

This gospel of Jesus Christ is the Word of deliverance with signs and wonders that confirm the Word of God. This same gospel inspires each of us to believe in God and to face the unknown path that God leads us to follow by a sheer and abiding faith. God uses this same gospel to help his ministers define the Word such that they discover, in God and in Him alone, a fulfillment that they have never known. This same Word of God inspires man to enter into a personal, intimate relationship with God that surpasses his relationship with the opposite sex.

Ministers of God are so moved upon by the Spirit of God that they dedicate their lives and lifestyles to Him. Therefore, this calling of God to the ministry permeates and influences everything a man of God endeavors to do. This call introduces zeal, strength, and vitality to man. It makes life interesting, exciting, and vibrant. It contains the seeds to prosperity and success in life because the call to the Christian ministry is really a call to a personal relationship with God. Whether the ministry is beset by success or failure, struggles or conflicts, God truly promises and is forever faithful to be with us. God's promise is comforting, assuring, and reassuring. God is faithful to provide for the goals and visions from the beginning to the end of Christian service. He makes us stewards of the gospel and servants to Him and man.

The man of God is led by God with such faith that if he decides to follow God into the deeper life of being anointed by God and of operating in the gifts of the Holy Spirit, he knows that, in this daring lifestyle, he must trust God above all else. His success and spiritual relationship with God is based on faith in God, the wisdom of God, good judgment, and intimate communication with God. He knows in his inner man, in his spirit, that his life depends on God's Spirit moving upon it. He knows that, beyond temporary satisfaction, the happiness and fulfillment of his family is based on their living according to God's Word. He knows that none other than *the Spirit of God must breathe upon* and be continuously on his ministry or he is doomed to failure.

Of course, he might establish a work of success and prosperity in his efforts and according to man's standards, but in his spirit and conscience, he knows that the deeper life in God must be full of God's Spirit. The word of God itself has persuaded him that, "It is not by might, nor by power, but by my spirit saith the Lord" (Zech. 4:6). Such is the call to the Christian ministry wherein God wants to develop every God-called, God-chosen man and woman, into "*Flames of Fire.*"

CHAPTER 1

GOD'S ULTIMATE FLAME OF FIRE

When we cultivate the mind of Christ and obey God, we become humble and can receive the Fire of the Holy Spirit. *Jesus, the Ultimate Flaming Fire of God*, sets the stage and demonstrates what He wants to do in our lives and ministries: To turn water into wine is one thing, but to raise the dead is another; to restore sanity to the insane is one thing, but to give life to the lifeless is another; to send forth healing to a critically ill person is one thing, but to send out the power of God to resurrect him who is in Satan's grasp by death's hand is another; to feed more than five thousand people is one thing, but to have the power to restore to life him who cannot eat because his mouth is shut in death is another; to cast out a legion of demons from the demon possessed is one thing, but to snatch a person from the victorious grasp of the demons as they dance around the chief demon, Death, is another. These miracles demonstrate the power of the anointing in Jesus' life and ministry and are equally valued. Neither time, nor place, nor person, diminishes His life or His ministry.

For illustration purposes, let us follow our chief example, Jesus Christ the Anointed One, in the story of Lazarus. Lazarus and his two sisters, Mary and Martha, are Jesus' intimate friends. So when

Lazarus becomes ill, his sisters send a message to Jesus: "'Lord, behold, he whom thou lovest is sick.' When Jesus heard that, He said, 'This sickness is not unto death, but for the glory of God, that the Son of God might be glorified thereby'" (John 11:3–4).

I pause to focus on a very important question: How did the sisters know where our Lord Jesus was? Whenever we are in trouble, God wants us to know that if we search diligently for Him as we would look for our lost wallet containing our monthly salary or for pure gold, we shall find Him. Jesus promised:

> Because he hath set his love upon me, therefore will I deliver him: I will set him on high, because he hath known my name. He shall call upon me, and I will answer him: I will be with him in trouble; I will deliver him and honour him. With long life will I satisfy him, and shew him my salvation.
> —Psalm 91:14–16

Mary and Martha were in a predicament; their brother was nearing death. They loved Jesus, knew His name, and witnessed the effects of His power. What other name or person should they call upon at this dreadful time in their lives? Who, other than Jesus, could deliver them out of these circumstances? The sisters' hearts were sincere, and they called upon the Anointed One. After all, in the God-inspired words of the psalmist, God promised to be with them in times of trouble. So they called, and Jesus heard their cry. Yet, He waited two days before coming to their rescue.

Our timing is not Jesus' timing, and we must rest in Him while we maintain our faith in His promises and wait patiently for Him to move in His timing. Our attitude can determine the answer or the desired outcome to our situation. If our faith is weak and we do not rest in Him, we shall miss the blessing(s). If our faith is strong, the likelihood of a positive outcome or deliverance is greater. God's ways are not our ways, and His thoughts are far above our thoughts. "For my thoughts are not your thoughts, neither are your ways my ways, saith the LORD. For as the heavens are higher than the earth, so are my ways higher than your ways, and my thoughts than your thoughts" (Isa. 55:8–9).

Jesus waited two days after receiving the news of Lazarus' life-threatening illness. The messenger returned to the sisters and stated that Jesus had personally received the news of their brother's illness. Yet Jesus did not come. Disappointing though this must have been for Lazarus' sisters, we must rest in the knowledge that Christ always knows what He is doing in our lives for our good and in our best interest. "What shall we then say to these things? If God be for us, who can be against us?" (Rom. 8:31). To express this sentiment in another way: "And we know that all things work together for good to them that *love God*, to them who are the called according to his purpose" (Rom. 8:28). God turned Lazarus and his sisters' crisis around for good and for God's glory so that Christ Himself would be glorified.

It is very important to realize that nothing happens to the child of God by chance or accident—no crisis, no loss, no gain. Nothing shall separate us from the love of God that is in Christ Jesus. God permits the tragedies that come into our lives. If we reflect on the righteous man Job, we will understand that God permits Satan, who is on His leash, to go only so far in our lives. God keeps Satan from destroying the souls of those who are living to glorify Him by their sanctified and regenerated lives.

Job lost his children, his livestock, and his crops, and his wife was estranged from him. Job's wife, who was influenced by Satan, suggested that he should curse God and die because of their suffering. Satan, who told God, "'But put forth thine hand now, and touch all that he hath, and he will curse thee to thy face.' And the LORD said unto Satan, 'Behold all that he hath is in thy power; only upon himself put not forth thine hand.' So Satan went forth from the presence of the LORD" (Job 1:11–12).

Why does Satan feel that he has studied our actions, attitudes, and thought patterns so well that he can dare God to put forth His hand to afflict us with loss or sickness, and we will curse God to His face? Observe Satan's audacity: "And Satan answered the LORD, and said, 'Skin for skin, yea, all that a man hath will he give for his life. But put forth thine hand now, and touch his bone and his flesh, and he will curse thee to thy face'" (Job 2:4–5). Satan, however, underestimated the power of God's instilled righteousness in a true child of God whose heart is right toward Him, whose heart is set upon God, the source of the child of God's provision.

Even though God allowed the illness, He did not afflict Job with sickness. Yet many error-prone children of God believe that, when we are sick, lose possessions, or experience a tragic event in our lives, it is the work of God. They do not understand or have forgotten the conversation between God and Satan. "And the LORD *said* unto Satan, 'Behold, he is in thine hand; but save his life'" (Job 2:6).

Job, though stricken with boils (sores) from the crown of his head to the soles of his feet, maintained his integrity and never cursed God. What an example for us today! If we are sincere in our relationship with God, we know that our past record of living as God's servant by faith in godly righteousness gets God's attention when we call upon Him. God promised that He would answer the call of the faithful. So Jesus, having answered the call of Mary and Martha, is now on the scene at Lazarus' tomb to do what is needed for those who have experienced an intimate, close *friendship* and *fellowship with Him* in their time of trouble.

Listen, if you will, to the heart of Martha as she greets Jesus: "Then said Martha unto Jesus, 'Lord, if thou hadst been here, my brother had not died. But I know, that even now, whatsoever thou wilt ask of God, God will give it thee'" (John 11:21–22). This might sound like Martha is rebuking or criticizing Jesus, but look beneath the surface to see what his grieving sister is saying from her heart. First, she is expressing faith in the anointing of the Holy Spirit of God upon Jesus, for she had witnessed the mighty works of God through His Son, Jesus. Second, she believes in Jesus for the sake of the works (miracles) of God. Third, she is saying, Because I know of your love for my brother, Lazarus, had you been here before death took him, you would have healed him by just speaking the word of healing or by laying on of hand. Fourth, because I know you and Mary knows you, and Lazarus knew you in intimate, open, vulnerable, defenseless friendship and communication, You would have saved my brother from death.

Are these not heartfelt expressions of faith? The power of life and death is in the tongue. We must speak life and healing into our lives if we are to overcome the mighty works of the Devil. We must act on our faith if we are to see and know the mighty presence of God in us. We must understand and recognize the unction of the Holy Spirit when He prompts our hearts to act on His behalf in ministering healing, deliverance, and freedom from Satan's grasp. We must recognize the voice of God from the Spirit in our ears. Can we know God's Voice, when He speaks to us? Yes! Yes! Jesus said so in John 10:2–5:

> But he that entereth by the door is the shepherd of the sheep. To him the porter openeth; and the sheep hear his voice: and he calleth his own sheep by name, and leadeth them out. And when he putteth forth his own sheep, he goeth before them, and the sheep follow him: for they know his voice. And a stranger will they not follow, but will flee from him: for they know not the voice of strangers.

Our Savior Jesus forcefully said, "They know his voice." How do we know His Voice?

1. We are in His fold.
2. He is the Chief Shepherd of shepherds.
3. He knows *each* of *us* by name.
4. We, who are in His flock, have been led in and out by Him into the pastures of life.
5. He has built a brook for us so that we can drink or consume His Word as the still waters.
6. When we have strayed, He moves heaven and hell to find us and bring us back into the fold.

7. He calls us by name while we are with Him in whatever way necessary to keep us with Him.

8. Though we stray, we return to Him in confession and repentance because we experience protection, nurturing, and nourishing of a kind that no one else can give.

9. In willingness of heart, we stay in the fold with the rest of our Christian sheep or we return with Him to the fold when He, Jesus, through the Holy Spirit, comes and finds us in the decadence of sin.

10. Therefore, we know His voice because we have learned it as we walked by faith wherever He led us.

11. We talk with Him in prayer and know in our hearts that we communicate with Jesus, because our spirit connected with His Spirit while we prayed.

12. There is no connection on earth like our communication, relationship, and fellowship with Him.

13. Hence, we *know* His voice, and we run from false shepherds because there is no other voice like Jesus'. There is no other endowment with power like the Holy Spirit's. There is no other person's love like the love of God. We know Jesus' voice, and we are sensitive enough to His Spirit to flee from the false prophets of Satan.

This chapter on God's Ultimate Flame of Fire, Jesus, is the most appropriate context in which to differentiate the person whom Satan has used and is using as an "angel of light." Paul gave a stern warning to the early New Testament church against false apostles and ministers. You might ask why, Cromwell, do you engage in discussion of this controversial and unpopular subject? The church of God, the true believers in Jesus Christ, has been attacked and defensive for too long. It is time that we develop offensive tactics to fight against the forces of evil. Before getting on the adversary's (Satan's) turf, we must be assured of God's timing and His leadership. I have the assurance of our Shelter, Refuge, Fortress, and Secret Place of the Most High that we have to approach this issue now and in the future.

Because we, God's *flames of fire*, have not dealt thoroughly with this important issue, many people have been led astray by the false doctrine and deceptive church strategies of Satan's false prophets. Observe God's word in 2 Corinthians 11:11–15:

> Wherefore? because I love you not? God knoweth. But what I do, that I will do, that I may cut off occasion from them which desire occasion; that wherein they glory, they may be found even as we. For such are *false apostles, deceitful workers*, transforming themselves into the apostles of Christ. And no marvel; for *Satan himself* is transformed into an angel of light. Therefore, it is no great thing if his ministers also be transformed as the ministers of righteousness; whose end shall be according to their works.

In speaking boldly against false ministers and false prophets, Paul demonstrated his love for those he served and for Jesus, his Lord. Therefore, his intention was to keep them from deceiving the true church. He was checkmating them. May we do the same because of our love for God, the church, and the people we serve! *The Living Bible* expresses 2 Corinthians 11:11–15 in these words:

> Why? Because I don't love you? God knows I do. But I will do it to cut out the ground from under the feet of those who boast that they are doing God's work in just the same way we are. God never sent these men at all; they are "phonies" who have fooled you into thinking they are Christ's apostles. Yet I am not surprised! Satan can change himself into an angel of light, so it is no wonder his servants can do it too, and seem like godly ministers. In the end they will get every bit of punishment their wicked deeds deserve.

Jesus, in warning us about false prophets, put it this way in Matthew 24:24: "For there shall arise false Christs, and false prophets, and shall shew great signs and wonders; insomuch that, if it were possible, they shall deceive the very elect."

I share with you lists of the signs of false ministers and false prophets as compiled in the *Dake's Annotated Reference Bible*,

King James Version. I would also strongly suggest that you examine each sign by reading the Scripture verses given:

SIXTEEN MARKS OF FALSE MINISTERS IN 2 CORINTHIANS:

1. Hold secret things of shame (4:2).
2. Walk in craftiness (4:2).
3. Handle Word deceitfully (4:2).
4. Walk and war after the flesh (10:3).
5. Look on outward appearance (10:7); compare 1 Samuel 16:7; Matthew 23:27–28.
6. Commend selves (10:12).
7. Compare selves to others (10:12–16).
8. Prey on works of others (10:15–16).
9. Greedy of income (11:7–12).
10. False: seek high office (11:13).
11. Deceitful workers (11:13).
12. Counterfeit apostleship (11:13).
13. Pose as righteous ministers (11:15).
14. Seek occasion to glory (11:12).
15. Boastful and self-exalting (11:18).
16. Destitute of apostolic signs (12:12).

34 MORE MARKS OF FALSE MINISTERS:

1. Lead men from God (Deut. 13:1–5).
2. Speak presumptuously (Deut. 18:20).
3. Propagate errors (Ps. 19:27; Isa. 3:12; Jer. 23:32).
4. Have no sense of righteousness (Isa. 19–20).
5. Teach lies (Isa. 9:14–16).
6. Destitute of light (Isa. 8:19–20).
7. Live like sinners (Isa. 28:7).
8. Ignorant of spiritual things (Isa. 29:10–11, 56:10–12; Jer. 2:8; Hosea 4:6).
9. Compromise truth (Isa. 30:10).
10. Greedy and lazy (Isa. 56:10–12).

11. Deal falsely (Jer. 6:13; Ezek. 22:27).
12. Do not pray (Jer. 10:21).
13. Destroy and scatter (Jer. 12:10, 23:1).
14. Preach lies (Jer. 14:13–16).
15. Commit adultery (Jer. 23:14).
16. Encourage sin (Jer. 23:14; Ezek. 13:22).
17. Deceitful (Jer. 48:10; Ezek. 13:10; Rom. 16:18; Eph. 4:14; Col. 2:4–8, 2 Tim. 3:6–13).
18. Sinful (Ezek. 34:2–3).
19. Liars (Jer. 23:14, Ezek. 13:19–22).
20. Selfish (Ezek. 34:2–3).
21. Unfaithful (Ezek. 34:2–3).
22. Covetous (Mic. 3:11).
23. Teach doctrines of men (Matt. 15:9).
24. Work iniquity (Matt. 7:15–22).
25. Blind (Matt. 15:14).
26. Cause divisions (Rom. 16:17; 1 Cor. 11:18; Phil. 1:15–16).
27. Corrupt truth (2 Cor. 2:17).
28. Teach doctrines of devils (1 Tim. 4:2).
29. Proud and perverse (1 Tim. 6:3–21; 2 Tim. 2:14–18; Titus 1:10–14).
30. Teach damnable heresies (2 Pet. 2:1, 2; 2 John 7–11).
31. Seared conscience (1 Tim. 4:2).
32. Deny Christ (2 Pet. 2:1; 1 John 4:1–6).
33. Consecrated to destroy Christianity (2 Pet. 2:1–19; Jude 4:41).
34. Hypocrisy (notes on Matt. 7:15, 23:1–33; Luke 11:35).

To defend ourselves and those we serve against the attacks of the Enemy, we have to "*Be* sober, *be* vigilant; because your adversary the devil, as a roaring lion, walketh about, seeking whom he may devour: Whom resist stedfast in the faith, knowing that the same afflictions are accomplished in your brethren that are in the world" (1 Pet. 5:8–9). First John 4:1–3 cautions:

Beloved, believe not every spirits but try the spirits whether they are of God: because many false prophets are gone out into the world. Hereby know ye the Spirit of God: Every spirit that confesseth that Jesus Christ is come in the flesh is of God: And every spirit that confessed not that Jesus Christ is come in the flesh is not of God: and this is that spirit of antichrist, whereof ye have heard it should come; and even now already is it in the world.

The attacks to steal, kill, and destroy the body of Christ and its leaders are by false prophets and false ministers. The time has come for us to lead an offensive strategic attack against this major stronghold of Satan in the church. We must take back ground that the Devil has taken or conquered. I am reminded that this was part, parcel, and seal of the ministry of Jesus, our Ultimate Flame of Fire.

The Pharisees and Sadducees of Jesus' day were used by Satan to destroy and conquer the sincere Jewish people who believed in God. John the Baptist called them "vipers." Matthew 3:7–8 says, "But when he saw many of the Pharisees and Sadducees come to his baptism, he said unto them, 'O generation of vipers, who hath warned you to flee from the wrath to come? Bring therefore fruits meet for repentance.'" You and I share the responsibility to continue what Jesus and John the Baptist began. We must accept the Great Commission to teach all nations. The true church must be knowledgeable of the weapons and tactics necessary to fight the Prince of the Air. Individuals anointed by the Holy Spirit will put on the whole armor of God and take their place on the battlefield.

Jesus knew that, to fulfill the *purpose* and to realize the *vision* that God instilled in His heart when He left the portals of heaven, He would have to suffer. In order to do this, He needed to be endowed with the power of God in God's anointing. He was living in just that anointing. His name, *Christos* in Greek, means "the Messiah, the Deliverer of His people." *Christos* also means "the Anointed One." Does that mean you are anointed as a child of God? Yes!

In fact, the second you were saved, the anointing of the Lord Jesus Christ became a part of you. The Anointed One, Jesus Christ in the person of the Holy Spirit, began to live in your heart, your spirit. So as a saved, called minister of Christ, you have the Anointed One in you. So, if you have been opposed to those who are sincerely known to operate in the anointing of Christ, you have been fighting that which is a major part of you. Even more importantly, you have been fighting Christ's Holy Spirit.

Nevertheless, each of us must function in the knowledge that we pay a tremendous price to operate and flow in the anointing of Jesus Christ. Not one of us knows the exact value or nature of this price. However, we do know that the price includes suffering, and with the suffering comes the strength for us to endure in the anointing. While paying the price, we must not give up, give in, or give out. "Let us not be weary in well doing: for in due season we shall reap, if we faint not" (Gal. 6:9). Proverbs 24:10 supports this assertion: "If thou faint in the day of adversity, thy strength is small."

Jesus knew the price His Father was asking Him to pay. Therefore, we are not disregarding any of His previous acts or works before His crucifixion, but we wish to focus on three outstanding examples of our suffering Savior's endurance because of God's anointing on Him. First, He had the anointing to be obedient to His Father, God. I sense deep in my spirit that this is an anointing we need to pray for. This we find in Hebrews 12:1–11:

> *Wherefore seeing* we are compassed about with so great a cloud of witnesses, *let us* lay aside every weight, and the sin which doth so easily beset us, and *let us* run with patience the race that is set before us. Looking unto Jesus the author and finisher of our faith; who for the joy that was set before him endured the cross, despising the shame, and is set down at the right hand of the throne of God. For *consider him* that endured such contradiction of sinners against himself, *lest*

ye be wearied and faint in you minds. Ye have not resisted unto blood, striving against sin. And ye have forgotten the exhortation which speaketh unto you as unto children, My son, *despise not* thou the chastening of the Lord, *nor faint* when thou art rebuked of him: for whom the Lord loveth he chasteneth, and scourgeth *every son* whom he receiveth. If ye endure chastening, God dealeth with you as with sons; for what son is he whom the father chasteneth not? But if ye be without chastisement, whereof *all are partakers*, then are ye bastards, and not sons. Furthermore we have had fathers of our flesh which corrected us, and we gave them reverence: *shall we not* much rather be in subjection unto the Father of spirits, and live? *For they* verily for a few days chastened us after their own pleasure; *but he* for our profit, *that* we might be partakers of his holiness. Now no chastening for the present seemeth to be joyous, but grievous: nevertheless *afterward* it yieldeth the peaceable fruit of righteousness unto them which are exercised thereby.

I believe Jesus learned obedience in the Garden of Olives during His prayers to God. Hebrews 5:8 states. "Though he were a Son, yet learned he obedience by the things which he suffered." Imagine this scene, and Jesus' words recorded by Luke in 22:39–44:

And he came out, and went, as he was wont, to the mount of Olives; and his disciples followed him. And when he was at the place, he said unto them, "Pray that ye enter not into temptation." And he was withdrawn from them about a stone's cast, and kneeled down and prayed, saying, "Father, *if thou be willing,* remove this cup from me: nevertheless *not my will, but thine, be done.*" And there appeared an angel unto him from heaven, strengthening him. And being in agony he prayed more earnestly: and his sweat was as it were great drops of blood falling down to the ground.

In the words: "Father, *if thou be willing,* remove this cup from me: nevertheless, *not my will but thine, be done,*" He agreed to obey His Father even unto suffering. Here was a determined act of obedience to God, the Father, to become the propitiation for our sins. Jesus sacrificed His life so that you and I could be saved. I'm reminded that, as we are anointed, our lives are anointed. Therefore, Jesus was anointed to suffer. We too are anointed and strengthened by God to suffer as is needed to fulfill that task/vision to which He has called us. We must walk in this anointing even as our most Ultimate Flame of Fire walked in His anointing to suffer.

The second anointing of Christ's suffering was His crucifixion. The apostle Paul was very much aware of this. So he said in Philippians 3:10: "*That I may know him*, and the power of his resurrection, and of the fellowship of his sufferings, being made conformable unto his death."

"The fellowship of Christ's suffering, being made conformable unto his death" is one of those crucial but unpopular areas with us. We want the power of Christ's or God's anointing without the suffering to obtain and operate in it. We want the acclaim of a great teacher or preacher without paying the price of quality time in the Word of God that expresses His mind and His will. We want the exceeding abundance of blessed prosperity in every way possible with all deliberate speed without an intimate relationship and fellowship with God in His Presence by persistent obedience to His will in our personal and professional lives. We desire the anointing of Christ without praying His Word to answer our petitions according to His will. We want to flow in the anointing and to see it work miracles in our lives and the lives of others without the drawing near to God so that He will draw near to us. "*Draw nigh* to God, and he will draw nigh to you" (James 4:8a). That's where the *fire* is. That's where the *flames* are. That's where the intensified heat of the anointing burns the sin out of man's heart so that he can come to the Ultimate Flame of Fire. We urgently desire God's best in our lives and ministries without sacrificing our secret sins. James 4:8b says, "Cleanse your hands, ye sinners; and purify your hearts, ye double minded."

Christ suffered the crucifixion in His anointing so that you and I could come to Him in confession and repentance of our unclean hands and heart. He did this so that we could be single-minded, with focused lives and hearts stayed on Jesus and what He has purposed in our lives.

Let me say without apology that sometimes the refiner's pot is required to purify us. This is required so that we never turn to sinful living or to our former lives when we had no knowledge of Jesus. This is required so that our own selfishness and selfish ways are burnt off, and we can put on Christ and His unselfish ways. First Peter 1:6–7 says it well:

> Wherein ye greatly rejoice, though now for a season, if need be, ye are in heaviness through manifold temptations: that the *trial of your faith*, being more precious than of gold that perisheth, though it be tried with fire, might be found unto praise and honour and glory at the appearing of Jesus Christ.

We are the gold of the Lord that must go through the fire. Hopefully, we will grow through the trials of our faith. We, as the gold of God, possess faith in Jesus in our hearts and in our spirits.

Depending on our knowledge of what the Lord is doing in our lives on this issue and how we bear the many and various trials, we can fail and just go through or we can become more mature in the Lord. Lack of knowledge is a terrible thing. What we don't know *can* hurt or even kill us. God said, "My people are destroyed for lack of knowledge" (Hosea 4:6a). This statement comes not as criticism but as an observation. Sometimes, as God's ministers, we are not aware that He allows the trials to prove us. He does this to purify us, to lop off things on or in us that would prevent our growth in Him. As the branches of Jesus Christ, we must be pruned to grow strong and energetic in the Lord.

Too many God-sent men and women have fallen by the wayside because they do not know God in this manner. Too many Christians of great abilities have lost their focus, determination, dedication, and faith in God and Christ because they misunderstand the hand of God in their lives. Many of them grew weak, weary in trial and adversity, and turned away from the Lord. The trial of our faith is a necessity so that God can grow us and promote us through the ranks of His natural and spiritual army to fight the echelons of demons commanded by the Devil. The General of generals, God through Jesus Christ and the Holy Spirit, will have the toughest and most well-prepared armed forces to defeat Satan and his military forces on earth. We cannot and should not be *absent without leave*. This must be understood!

The trial of our faith is required and necessary; the test must be passed to the utmost of our ability. The Refiner's (God's) fire is a must in our Christian journey. It must occur if we are going to be the most intense flames of fire under the protection, nurture, nourishing, and hiding place of the wings of the Ultimate Flame of Fire, Jesus. Trials of our faith, the intense heat of the Refiner's fire, cause us to put off the various kinds of weights that hold us down and back from doing what the Lord has told us and called us to do. Frequently these weights can be possessions, but our lives consist not in the things we possess. The weights could be various kinds of prestige or status, and we have to be careful that we don't abuse and misuse our position over others. The weights could be various kinds of power. This, too, should never be abused or misused. We must be aware of the snares and the pitfalls of evil. Proverbs 3:1–6 in *The Living Bible* speaks to the three P's: possession, prestige, and power:

> My Son, never forget the things I've taught you. If you want a satisfying life, closely follow my instructions. Never forget to be truthful and kind. Hold these virtues tightly. Write them deep within your heart. If you want favor with both God and man, and a reputation for good judgment and common sense, then trust the Lord completely; don't ever trust yourself. In everything you do, put God first, and He will direct you and crown your efforts with success.

Within the midst of our favor with man, we should never allow what they say to or about us or think of us to deter us, especially when we are assured of doing God's will. Too often and too long we have allowed the opinions of men to hold or prevent us from doing what God demands. "And fear not them which kill the body, but are not able to kill the soul: but rather fear Him which is able to destroy both soul and body in hell" (Matt. 10:28). Neither possessions, prestige, nor natural power can save, edify, or equip us to do the works of Christ. Zechariah 4:6 reminds us of this truth: "Then he answered and spake unto me, saying, 'This is the word of the LORD unto Zerubbabel, saying, Not by might, nor by power, but by my spirit, saith the LORD of hosts.'" In my spirit and in my heart, if God gives me power with Him, power with man will come. If I do His will as His Word expresses His mind and will, the possessions, prestige, and power will come. He has promised as much in His Word, the Bible. Therefore, my real concern is having more of the power of Christ in me, the hope of glory, to do His will. My real concern is maintaining a position of humility and trust, reverencing Him in the fear of God, as He gives me prestige and position. These are to be used to influence and motivate a person to the saving knowledge of Jesus Christ, our Savior.

So what does the crucifixion of Christ mean? If the Cross of Jesus means anything, it defines *self-denial* so that this sinful, wicked, corrupt world can be saved. As a result of salvation, we are edified, built up in the body of Jesus Christ. Therefore, we are equipped, as a result of maturity in Christ, to be the spiritually strong, prepared military forces of God to defeat the works of Satan. We deny ourselves to put off the works of the carnal mind and carnality. We mortify the deeds of the flesh, and we live so others can live. We put to death the deeds of our fleshly bodies that war against the Spirit of God and our spirit.

Romans 8:1–5 illustrates very well our deliverance from the law of sin in the flesh that imprisoned and therefore held us captive to do the works of fleshly nature, the world, and the Devil.

> There is therefore now no condemnation to them which are in Christ Jesus, who walk not after the flesh, but after the Spirit. For the law of the Spirit of life in Christ Jesus hath made me free from the law of sin and death. For what the law could not do, in that it was weak through the flesh, God sending his own Son in the likeness of sinful flesh, and for sin, condemned sin in the flesh: that the righteousness of the law might be fulfilled in us, who walk not after the flesh, but after the Spirit. For they that are after the flesh do mind the things of the flesh, but they that are after the Spirit the things of the Spirit.

The following verses of Romans 8:6–13 contrast being carnally minded and spiritually minded within the context of our mortifying (putting to death) and denying the works of our fleshly nature.

> For to be carnally minded is death; but to be spiritually minded is life and peace. Because the carnal mind is enmity against God: for it is not subject to the law of God, neither indeed can be. So then they that are in the flesh cannot please God. But ye are not in the flesh, but in the Spirit, if so be that the Spirit of God dwell in you. Now if any man have not the Spirit of Christ, he is none of his. And if Christ be in you, the body is dead because of sin; but the Spirit is life because of righteousness. But if the Spirit of him that raised up Jesus from the dead dwell in you, he that raised up Christ from the dead shall also quicken your mortal bodies by his Spirit that dwelleth in you. Therefore, brethren, we are debtors, not to the flesh, to live after the flesh. For if ye live after the flesh, ye shall die: but if ye through the Spirit do mortify the deeds of the body, ye shall live.

So in dying to self, we put on the love of God for our fellow man and ourselves. In dying to self, we become Christ centered, not self-centered. In dying to self, we put off greed and take on an enthusiasm and passion for the things of God. In dying to self, our selfish purposes are deleted, and we take up Christ's purposes for our lives. In dying to self, our goals are dissipated, and we become possessors of His goals for us. Christ's vision for us becomes our vision. In dying to self, we no longer seek His hand only for what we want, but we seek His face and His righteousness for what God wants for us. Jesus said, "But seek ye *first* the kingdom of God, and his righteousness; and *all these things* shall be added unto you" (Matt. 6:33).

In dying to self, we put off wanting our way, one of the greatest forms of selfishness, and we take up consistently wanting His way. In dying to self, we put off loving only ourselves. In dying to self, we destroy the deeds of the flesh of lust, the world, and the Devil, and we put on the deeds of Christ within us. In dying to self, we lose our selfish pride and pomposity, and we recognize who we are in Him, God our Father. "Then said Jesus unto his disciples, If any man will come after me, let him *deny himself,* and *take up his cross*, and *follow Me.* For whosoever will save his life shall lose it: and whosoever will lose his life for my sake shall find it" (Matt. 16:24–25). This is the way of *the* cross.

Christ suffered emotionally. Crying is strong evidence that something emotional (feeling) is going on within the weeper. Listen to this if you will: "Who in the days of his flesh, when he had offered up prayers and supplications with strong crying and tears unto him that was able to save him from death, and *was heard* in that he feared; Though he were a Son, yet learned he obedience by the things which he suffered; and *being made perfect,* he became the author of eternal salvation unto all them that obey him" (Heb. 5:7–9).

Remember the scene of Christ's suffering and agony in the garden in the Mount of Olives.

> And he was withdrawn from them about a stone's cast, and kneeled down, and prayed, saying, Father, *if thou be willing*, remove this cup from me; nevertheless *not my will, but thine, be done.* And there appeared an angel unto him from heaven,

1 8

strengthening him. And being in agony he prayed more earnestly; and his sweat was *as it were* great drops of blood falling down to the ground.

—Luke 22:41–44

What an emotional struggle against the forces of evil in their attempt to kill Him! It brought tears and caused His sweat to become diluted with blood. Satan and his demons were attempting to kill Jesus while He prayed. Their purpose was to thwart God's prophecy in Genesis 3:15: "And I will put enmity between thee and the woman, and between thy seed and her seed; it shall bruise thy head, and thou shalt bruise his heel."

Satan knew that Jesus was the person who would injure him as he had never been injured before. Jesus was, and still is, Satan's *number one* enemy. Therefore, he brought everything to bear to prevent Him from achieving His (Jesus'*)* *vision* on the cross. This great struggle against evil required the Lord's utmost emotions combined with His desire to obey God's will for Him. Hence, He learned obedience by these things that He suffered. He gave His will over to God's will. Jesus maintained God's purpose as His purpose. Jesus implemented God's vision. This struggle so affected His emotions and caused such mental strain that it was shown in His sweat. But listen to His words. I pray that, if the time and situation ever became necessary, you and I will cry the same words with determination, "Nevertheless, *not my will but thine be done.*" God sent an angel from heaven to strengthen Him.

This should impact us emotionally, psychologically, and spiritually. Christ knew who He was, whose he was, and what His purpose in the earth and spiritual realm was; He also knew that His vision was really God's vision for Him, so He withstood His suffering. Similarly, my brothers and sisters in the Lord, God's flames of fire, our victory comes *after* our obedience. Our possessions, prestige, and position are the results of our learning obedience to God's will in the midst of suffering. Realizing our potential and increasing our faith is dependent on our being willingly obedient in spite of the consequences.

> *Let* this mind be in you, which was also in Christ Jesus: who, being in the form of God, thought it not robbery to be equal with God: but *made himself* of no reputation, and took upon him the form of a servant, and *was made* in the likeness of men: and *being* found in the fashion as a man, *he humbled himself*, and became obedient unto death, even the death of the cross.
>
> —Philippians 2:5–8

When Jesus healed the leprous skin of lepers, it was bringing new skin into life for them; it was an exhibition of the power of the Resurrection! In Him was the power of resurrection. He was the Resurrection and the Life, and He used it for our sake to *confirm His Word*. When Jesus restored the High Priest's servant's severed ear that Simon cut off, He was bringing back to life that which was dead, an ear separated from the body. For what is death but a separation from life? When the *Ultimate Anointed*, Jesus Christ, rose from the dead, He did it by His resurrection power.

Jesus is God's Ultimate Firebrand. He is God's Ultimate Anointed. He is God's Ultimate Flame of Fire. God's Ultimate Flame of Fire desires to develop us into flames of fire, firebrands for Him. He desires us to be effective in every area of Christian ministry and work under the power of His anointing.

CHAPTER 2

THE FIRE OF
THE HOLY SPIRIT

A s one seeks God's face and yields to the fire of His Holy
Spirit, God will anoint His ministers so that they become
firebrands of His Spirit. The anointing of the Holy Spirit will
enable us to do the works of Christ in His church and with
His people. The fire of the Holy Spirit is a greater intensity of
God's anointing on His chosen, those He can trust to handle
and minister this anointing to others righteously, charitably, and
without abuse or misuse. These will protect Christ's anointing
on them at all costs.

They know that it is their greatest affection that influences
every thing else in their lives. Proverbs 4:23, The Living Bible,
says: "Above all else, guard your affections. For they influence
everything else in your life." This anointing is none other than
God Himself within us, abiding in our spirit to do greater
exploits for Him. Did not Jesus say, "Verily, verily, I say unto
you, *he that believeth* on me, the works that I do shall he do also;
and greater works than these shall be do; because I go unto my
Father" (John 14:12).

Jesus, at the time of His baptism by John the Baptist, experienced a greater baptism than water baptism. He experienced
the baptism of the Holy Spirit as God's Spirit descended and

lighted upon Him. "And Jesus, when he was baptized, went up straightway out of the water: and, lo, the heavens were opened unto him, and he saw the Spirit of God descending like a dove, and lighting upon him: and lo a voice from heaven, saying, 'This is my beloved son, in whom I am well pleased'" (Matt. 3:16–17).

During the winter months, we like to light the oak wood in the fireplace. Once the fire is started the wood burns. As the wood burns more intensely, the heat increases and the flames leap higher. Even if the light in the room is off, there is light from the fire in the fireplace because of the burning logs. So is the baptism of the Holy Spirit, Christ's anointing in and on His ministers to reprove the world of sin, and of righteousness and of judgment. Jesus said of the Holy Spirit, the Comforter's coming,

> Nevertheless, I tell you the truth; *It is expedient for you* that I go away: *for if* I go not away: the Comforter will not come unto you; *but if I* depart, I will send him unto you. And *when he is come,* he will reprove the world of sin, and of righteousness, and of judgment: of sin, because they believe not on me; of righteousness, because I go to my Father, and ye see me no more; of judgment, because the prince of this world is judged.
>
> —John 16:7–11

Furthermore, let's look at the words "lighting upon him" in Matthew 3:16. When a lit match touches paper, it starts a burning flame; the burning match causes the paper to burn. Similarly, the Holy Spirit of God works in us. The Holy Spirit, the anointing, is the source of the burning just as the match is the source of the natural flame. The Holy Spirit burning within us lights the work for God: to preach the gospel and to save people of all races, ethnicities, creeds, and denominations by the thousands, even the millions. God's Spirit, Christ's Spirit, the Comforter, the Holy Spirit is within us to destroy the bonds of Satan from minds, souls, and spirits.

The Holy Spirit, the fire of God within us, abides in us and on our lives to remove the blocks or barriers around our thinking so we can see the grace and love of God in Christ Jesus. The Holy Spirit of Christ's divine life overflowing in us and on us destroys the sin in our hearts and replaces our old hearts with new ones bent toward God and His righteousness. The burning, the flame of God, is activated by our faith when we teach, preach, and operate in the gifts of the Spirit to save others, so that they will not possess a spirit of fear, but of power, love, and a sound mind. The Holy Spirit, the Fire of God, comes to save each person, to heal him of sicknesses and disease so that God, as a result of his faith in Christ Jesus, will make him whole. The Bible says, "And Jesus went about all Galilee, teaching in their synagogues, and preaching the gospel of the kingdom, and healing all manner of sickness and all manner of disease among the people" (Matt. 4:23). In Matthew 10:1, He gave this same power to the disciples: "And when he had called unto him his twelve disciples, he *gave them power* against unclean spirits, *to cast them out*, and *to heal* all manner of sickness and all manner of disease." Jesus passed the power of the Holy Spirit to His disciples to perform even greater works than He had performed during His life on earth: "Verily, verily, I say unto you, he that believeth on me, the works that I do shall he do also; and greater *works* than these shall he do; because I go unto my Father" (John 14:12).

Psalm 104:4 shows God's work in His glory and power on His ministers who would become flaming fires for God. These would be burning with the zeal of God according to applicable knowledge of God's Word and operating in the gifts of the Holy Spirit and in the Spirit of God, for to do otherwise is to act in the flesh or under the influence of some other spirit. To be most effective for our *King of Kings*, we must operate in the *appropriate office of ministry to which God has called us*. He gives us greater anointing and power for our appropriate ministry in our correct office of prophet, apostle, evangelist, pastor, or teacher. This is where our anointing is most effective.

"Who maketh his angels spirits; his ministers a flaming fire" (Ps. 104:4). In this verse God shows His work in glory. Our crucified and resurrected Savior, Jesus Christ, is alive and sits on His throne at the right hand of God making intercessory prayers so that we, His ministers and children, will conform to doing not His permissive will, but His perfect will. Doing God's perfect will ignites us as flames of fire.

Exodus 14:21–22 describes Moses as an example of the flaming fire of God on one of His ministers who yields his will to God's will:

> And Moses stretched out his hand over the sea; and the LORD caused the sea to go back by a strong east wind all that night, and made the sea dry land, and the waters were divided. And the children of Israel went into the midst of the sea upon the dry ground: and the waters were a wall unto them on their right hand and on their left.

This miracle by faith parallels the gift of faith in the New Testament. As Moses operated with the gift of faith, the fire of God in and on him did mighty exploits for God.

As we recall, Moses had been in the immediate presence of God when he saw the *Flame of Fire* in the burning bush:

> And the angel of the LORD appeared unto him in a flame of fire out of the midst of the bush: and he looked, and, behold, the bush burned with fire, and the bush was not consumed. And Moses said, "I will now turn aside, and see this great sight, why the bush is not burnt." And when the LORD saw that he turned aside to see, *God called* unto him out of the midst of the bush, and said, "Moses, Moses." And he said, "Here am I." And he said, "Draw not nigh hither: put off thy shoes from off thy feet, for the place whereon thy standest is holy ground."
>
> —Exodus 3:2–5

As we see here, we need a personal, close encounter with God to position ourselves to get continuous direction for our lives. In other words, continuous, intimate fellowship with the *Flame of Fire, God*, will cause us to burn in our spirits, and out of

His Spirit, to do His will in power. Get around the Flame! Get around the Flame! Get around the Flame!

Another example of one of God's flames of fire in action is Elijah on Mt. Carmel. Elijah is engaged in spiritual warfare, a battle that, nevertheless, takes place in the natural realm of the earth. Elijah is in intense opposition against the forces of Satan, Jezebel's four hundred and fifty prophets of the groves. This battle between Elijah and the false prophets would determine the people's choice of false-idol gods or of the One and Only Living God.

> And Elijah said unto all the people, Come near unto me. And all the people came near unto him. And he repaired the altar of the LORD that was broken down. And Elijah took twelve stones, according to the number of the tribes of the sons of Jacob, unto whom the word of the LORD came, saying, Israel shall be thy name: And with the stones he built an altar in the name of the LORD: and he made a trench about the altar, as great as would contain two measures of seed. And he put the wood in order, and cut the bullock in pieces, and laid him on the wood, and said, "Fill four barrels with water, and pour it on the burnt sacrifice, and on the wood." And he said, "Do it the second time." And they did it the second time. And he said, "Do it the third time." And they did it the third time. And the water ran round about the altar; and he filled the trench also with water. And it came to pass at the time of the offering of the evening sacrifice, that Elijah the prophet came near, and said, "LORD God of Abraham, Isaac, and of Israel, let it be known this day that thou art God in Israel, and that I am thy servant, and that I have done all these things at thy word. Hear me, O LORD, hear me, that this people may know that thou art the LORD God, and that thou hast turned their heart back again." Then the fire of the LORD fell, and consumed the burnt sacrifice, and the wood, and the stones, and the dust, and licked up the water that was in the trench. And when all the people saw it, they fell on their faces: and they said, "The LORD, he is the God; the LORD, he is the God." And Elijah said unto them, "Take the

prophets of Baal; let not one of them escape." And they took them: and Elijah brought them down to the brook Kishon, and slew them there.

—1 Kings 18:30–40

Elijah, a man of God, under the power of the flaming fire anointing, prayed to God to show His signs and wonders to confirm the Word of God to save Israel from demonic, cultic worship of Satan which was led by 450 false prophets. This Flaming Fire prophet knew the power of prayer. He had been constantly in the presence of God in quality time of fellowship. He knew by the faith in his heart what God could do because of his personal intimate lifestyle of fellowship with our God, a Consuming Fire. Get close to the Fire of God! Get close to the Fire of God! Get close to the Fire of God! God gave the victory because Elijah was close to God, The Fire, in fellowship.

We must view Jesus, our Savior, as *God's Greatest Flame of Fire* and minister for God. God gave Jesus His power when John the Baptist baptized Him. "And Jesus, when he was baptized, went up straightway out of the water: and, lo, the heavens were opened unto him, and he saw the Spirit of God descending like a dove, and *lighting upon* him: and lo a voice from heaven, saying, this is my beloved Son, in whom I am well pleased" (Matt. 3:16–17). Fire touches an intended object and sets it aflame; the Spirit of God lit upon Jesus to give Him the glory, power, and strength to enable Him to withstand the forty days and forty nights of fasting. The Spirit of God activated the Word of God within Jesus to speak it with flaming power, to resist the temptations or snares of Satan. These attempted snares were lusts of the flesh, pride of life, and lust of the eye. These are the main umbrellas under which all sins fall. Adam and Eve lost their positions, power, and possessions in the Garden of Eden because of their disobedience, a sin.

Baptized of God with the Holy Ghost and with fire, Jesus was able to endure being tempted, like as we are; yet He did not sin. If we are to overcome the intense temptations of Satan—the lust of the flesh, the lust of the eye, and the pride of life, we must undergo baptism, not only with the Holy Ghost but also with fire. We need the greater strength of God to withstand the persecution of the godly, the trials of life and tribulations that sometimes come when we least expect them. We must never think that, because God heavily anoints us, we are invincible. For the Word of God proclaims, "Wherefore let him that thinketh he standeth take heed lest he fall. There hath no temptation taken you but such as is common to man: but God is faithful, who will not suffer you to be tempted above that ye are able; but will with the temptation make a way to escape, that ye may be able to bear it" (1 Cor. 10:12–13).

Our task then becomes, when we are tempted, to look for God's way to escape the temptation since we know that God will make an escape route for us. This we must do even though we are the anointed of God. Otherwise, when the Devil sets a snare for us, unless we take God's way of escape, he will catch us.

We must recognize that, as God's anointed vessels, we are at His disposal, and we are the ones Satan tempts most often and most intensely. Satan's plan is to cause us to fall. He is after the Word in us, our faith in our Father God, our anointing, and gifts of the Spirit. The bottom line is that Satan is after our ministries. So we need not only God's baptism of the Holy Ghost, but we also need the baptism of the fire of the Holy Spirit, the heaviest anointing, to enable us to endure and to be faithful to God.

Why is this necessary? What a great question! I refer us to Ezekiel 22:30–31 to discuss this question:

> And I sought for a man among them, that should make up the hedge, and stand in the gap before me for the land, that I should not destroy it: but I found none. Therefore, have I poured out mine indignation upon them; I consumed them with the fire of my wrath: their own way have I recompensed upon their heads, *saith the Lord* GOD.

We, God's ministers, are those that He called to lead His church, parts of Him of the whole body as a hedge that stands in the gap for the peoples of the earth.

Ephesians 4:16 speaks of us in the fivefold ministry as joined together: "From whom the whole body fitly joined together and compacted by that which every joint supplieth, according to the effectual working in the measure of every part, maketh increase of the body unto the edifying of itself in love." We proclaim the Word of God by our preaching, teaching, and lifestyle as God's interventionists, vessels of God that He uses to save mankind from destruction. As the hedge, standing in the gap, we are like God's bridge that helps man to cross from the side of Satan to the side of Jesus Christ for salvation and deliverance from sin and deadly diseases. We are the anointed in the power of God applied to man's ills.

If we define "*save*" as the root word for "salvation" and look at its original Greek meaning, "*salvation*" means to save, heal, deliver, make whole. Salvation is God's intervention that prevents man from ruining his life and the lives of others. When God saves a person, He intervenes and prevents the alcoholic from killing himself with alcoholic beverages. Christ Jesus coming into a person's heart by the Holy Spirit prevents the potential murderer from killing others. He prevents the prostitute and her saved, married lover from ruining and causing a broken home for his wife and children. Christ Jesus' incoming to the drug pusher's heart intervenes and prevents him from ruining the lives of other pushers, and their customers, the drug users. Salvation, by God's grace through faith, prevents the abusive wife, the abusive husband, the child abuser, and the seller of pornography from ruining others' lives. We, as God's flaming fires, His ministers, have a grave and vital responsibility as the vessels of intervention even as Jesus was in His ministry on earth.

We must make ourselves available and accessible to God to sound the trumpet of alarm with the gospel of Jesus Christ. God holds us responsible, and we must assume our responsibility or risk having righteous and unrighteous men's blood on our hands. God gave us this awesome task when He called us to ministry. We are God's watchmen standing in the gap, as told in Ezekiel 33:1–7:

> Again the word of the LORD came unto me, saying, "Son of man, speak to the children of thy people, and say unto them, 'When I bring the sword upon the land, if the people of the land take a man of their coasts, and set him for their watchman. If when he seeth the sword come upon the land, he blow the trumpet, and warn the people; then whosoever heareth the sound of the trumpet, and taketh not warning; if the sword come, and take him away, his blood shall be upon his own head. He heard the sound of the trumpet, and took not warning; his blood shall be upon him. But he that taketh warning shall deliver his soul. But if the watchman see the sword come, and blow not the trumpet, and the people be not warned; if the sword come, and take any person away from among them, he is taken away in his iniquity; but his blood will I require at the watchman's hand.' So thou, O son of man, I have set thee a watchman unto the house of Israel; therefore thou shalt hear the word at my mouth and warn them from me."

It behooves us to make our calling and election sure by faith, obedience, and endurance. God continuously nourished Christ Jesus' Flame. Christ always went to the source, God, for fuel. He did this persistently by getting away from those He served and spending quality time in solitude with God. "And straightway Jesus constrained his disciples to get into a ship, and to go before him unto the other side, while he sent the multitudes away. And when he had sent the multitudes away, he went up into a mountain apart to pray: and when the evening was come, he was there alone" (Matt. 14:22–23). The key to Christ's power over Satan before the crucifixion was His private meditation and prayer time with God.

We also must seek God's face first, rather than His hand of provision, in order to be flames of fire, to conquer Satan with Christ-given authority in our lives and ministries. Christ Jesus has already given us this power in His name accompanied by His anointing on us.

> And the seventy returned again with joy, saying, "Lord, even the devils are subject unto us through thy name." And He said unto them, "I beheld Satan as lightning fall from heaven. Behold, I give unto you power to tread on serpents and scorpions, and over all the power of the enemy: and nothing shall by any means hurt you."
>
> —Luke 10:17–19

We must draw near to Christ, whose countenance is as the sun. "And he had in his *right hand* seven stars: and out of his *mouth* went a sharp twoedged [sic] sword: and his countenance was as the sun shineth in his strength" (Rev. 1:16). Our becoming like Christ, filled with the fire of God, requires us to draw as near to Christ as possible. The provisions of God will come in the midst of our drawing closer to Him in seeking His face and His presence. We draw nearer to God during quality time with Him.

In our quiet quality time with God, the study of His Word is of utmost importance. Of course, this time should also include our praise and worship of our great God who inhabits our individual time with Him even as He inhabits corporate worship. My quiet time with God in prayer, praise, and worship not only gives me answers to crucial problems, but God also reveals Himself, shares revelatory knowledge, and vision and refreshes the anointing on me to face whatever circumstances, situations, and problems of the day. The victory is in the praise and worship of God. These mend our spirits from heart brokenness, disappointment, and rejection that are occupational hazards of being a child of God first and then a minister. Herein, I have found some of my greatest victories in renewing my spirit by putting on the garment of praise for the spirit of heaviness or depression. Again, the victory is in praising God.

An imminent attack by the Moabites, Ammonites, and others intimidated King Jehoshaphat and Judah and Jerusalem. They anticipated defeat because they were greatly outnumbered. Yet King Jehoshaphat realized that they alone were not the source of their spiritual or natural victory, so he and the people prayed, fasted, praised, and worshipped God. As a result, God spoke a sharpshooter's prophecy through Jahaziel. The prophecy was that they would win. "Be not afraid nor dismayed by reason of this great multitude; for the battle is not yours but God's" (2 Chron. 20:15). God reinforced this word for their future victory by and in Him alone. "Ye shall not need to fight in this battle: set yourselves, stand ye still, and see the salvation of the LORD with you, O Judah and Jerusalem: fear not, nor be dismayed; to morrow [sic] go out against them: for the LORD will be with you" (2 Chron. 20:17).

God later said in 2 Chronicles 20:20 through King Jehoshaphat, "Hear me, Oh Judah, and ye inhabitants of Jerusalem; Believe in the LORD your God, so shall ye be established; believe his prophets, so shall ye prosper." The people with their leader and the praise team worshiped God as they went to the place of battle depending on the Lord God and believing in Him for their security, believing the word of their prophets for prosperity. The Moabites and Ammonites in confusion with the others turned against each other in battle until they had killed each other to the last one. God gave the victory at the place of battle because the king and the people had faith in Him and His Word to them through His minister, a flame of fire. Because King Jehoshaphat and the people chose praise and worship over confusion and lamentations in the midst of what seemed like an imminent disaster, they were victorious.

Jesus' preparation for the daily battles as well as spiritual warfare was prayer.

> And straightway Jesus constrained his disciples to get into a ship, and to go before him to the other side, while he sent the multitudes away. And when he had sent the multitudes away, he went up into a mountain apart to pray: and when the evening was come, he was there alone.
>
> —Matthew 14:22–23

This is an important example set by the greatest Flaming Fire of God, Jesus, because He drew away from the crowd to spend quality time alone with God. Our Lord knew that ministry to others causes the outputting of physical, emotional, and spiritual energy to input into others the fruit of the Word so that they can bear fruit also. Because of this continuous, effective outpouring into others, however, God requires our spiritual refreshing and renewal so that we can be consistent and persistent in this great work of God through us.

The Lord Jesus often retired alone with God from the world for meditation and prayer. His private prayer life was the key to His absolute authority and defeat of Satan in His walk with God. This was the secret of His public and private power. It was in prayer that He received more power and fire of the Holy Spirit. In prayer, He received a fresh anointing of the *Holy Spirit* for His daily work. He used the same methods to acquire and maintain power that we need to minister with the fire of the Holy Spirit.

An example of Jesus ministering in the fire of the Holy Spirit was His healing of the woman who had a twelve-year issue of blood. Of course, this lady had tremendous faith in Jesus and real expectancy for her miracle. She said, "If I may touch but his clothes, I shall be whole" (Mark 5:28). Notice that she did not expect partial healing, for she stated: "I shall be whole." What an illustration of faith! She touched the Great Divine Healer's clothes and immediately the fountain of her blood was dried up, and she felt in her body that she was healed of that plague (Mark 5:29).

And Jesus, immediately knowing in himself that virtue had gone out of him, turned him about in the press, and said, "Who touched my clothes?" And his disciples said unto him, "Thou seest the multitude thronging thee, and sayest thou, 'Who touched me?'" And He looked round about to see her that had done this thing. But the woman fearing and trembling, knowing what was done in her, came and fell down before him, and told him all the truth. And he said unto her, "Daughter, thy faith hath made thee whole; go in peace, and be whole of thy plague."

—Mark 5:30–34

If we expect Jesus to do great things in us and for us, faith without doubt must be present in us for what we need and expect from Him even as the plagued woman applied this principle of faith. Faith without doubt is necessary for us to demonstrate the gifts of the Spirit and to get answers to our prayers.

Jesus, the Flaming Fire of God, with absolute authority and faith, used His power to heal all kinds of sicknesses and diseases believing that Father God who did the works through Him would heal with virtue (power), if only the person who needed the miracle would believe and receive from God.

Jesus said, "Thy faith hath made thee whole; go in peace, and be whole of the plague" (Mark 5:34). Jesus spoke of wholeness twice. Let us look at this reinforced completeness ministered by the Savior and Healer of all our diseases. Salvation and wholeness are synonymous in Scripture with our view of the Greek meaning of *soteria.* Therefore, when Jesus said, "Go in peace," He was speaking to her of the inner peace of salvation. When He spoke to her wholeness of the plague, He was speaking to her wholeness and the complete healing of her body. Therefore, God can provide salvation and healing of a person's soul and body at the same time.

I believe that, in these days and in the future, we shall see and experience more of this in the church as God manifests more of His glory and power. The glory and power of God will be shown not just through a few of God's war front generals as we know them today, but it will also be passed down to other men and women of God as they are obedient to Him and flow in sensitivity with His Spirit. We have heard and read of a few of God's flaming fires whose services are so filled with God's cloud of glory that the people in attendance are healed, delivered, and saved in their seats before and during the services. We have heard and read of God's power, manifested through these vessels of God, that has saved and healed people as they stood outside the meeting places and at their home prior to and during these services. However, God will shine forth His radiant anointing more abundantly among other ministers who will make themselves accessible to God to do what He will in and outside His church among the people of the earth. Did not Jesus say, "And the gospel must *first* be published among all nations" (Mark 13:10). "And this gospel of the kingdom shall be *preached in all the world* for a witness unto all nations; and then shall the end come" (Matt. 24:14).

As I write, more of God's minister servants are preaching and teaching on the anointing of Jesus Christ and the inner and outer working of this creative power of Christ, the Anointed One. The Word of this good news, the gospel of God's Messiah, the one who delivers people from their sins, diseases, sicknesses, habits, and corruptions, must be proclaimed. This glorious message of God must be propagated throughout the earth and the church:

> For the perfecting of the saints, for the work of the ministry, for the edifying of the body of Christ: Till we all come in the unity of the faith, and of the knowledge of the Son of God, unto a perfect man, unto the measure of the stature of the fulness of Christ: That we henceforth be no more children, tossed to and fro, and carried about with every wind of doctrine, by the sleight of men, and cunning craftiness, whereby they lie in wait to deceive; But speaking the truth in love, may grow up into him in all things, which is the head, even Christ: from whom the whole body fitly joined together

and compacted by that which every joint supplieth, according
to the effectual working in the measure of every part, maketh
increase of the body unto the edifying of itself in love.

—Ephesians 4:12–16

Jesus, the greatest Flaming Fire of God, inspired the church
to edify itself in love, healed people, and forgave the sin of man.
"And behold they brought to Him a man sick of the palsy, lying
on a bed, and Jesus seeing their faith said unto the sick of the
palsy; 'Son, be of good cheer; thy sins be forgiven thee'" (Matt.
9:2). "But that ye may know that the Son of man hath power
on earth to forgive sins, (then saith He to the sick of the palsy,)
'Arise, take up thy bed, and go unto thine house.' And he arose,
and departed to his house" (Matt. 9:6–7). Again, we see salvation and healing or deliverance occurring at the same time in the
ministry of Jesus operating in the gifts of the Spirit. We often say
that to be a Christian means to be Christ like or like Jesus. If this
is so, and it is, then we have to realize that Jesus our Lord and
Savior operated in all the gifts of the Spirit. He also wants us to
be His flaming fire ministers who operate in the gifts of the Holy
Ghost.

Lastly, I refer us to the Spirit's imparting the fire of God on
the New Testament church of which we are a part today:

And when the day of Pentecost was fully come, they were
all with one accord in one place. And suddenly there came a
sound from heaven as of a rushing mighty wind, and it filled
all the house where they were sitting. And there appeared unto
them cloven tongues like as of fire, and it sat upon each of
them. And they were all filled with the Holy Ghost, and began
to speak with other tongues, as the Spirit gave them utterance.

—Acts 2:1–4

This experience of God's amazing grace in establishing His
church for the work that is before us is far from being over. After
the crucifixion of Christ, the Anointed One, God anointed
His leaders with His power and glory. This was done with the

mighty rushing of the Holy Spirit, and Christ, whose voice is as the sound of many waters, who wants us to be so filled with His Spirit and so anointed by Him that we cannot help but know the exceeding greatness of His power according to the working of His mighty power. Christ our Lord, God our Father, and the Holy Spirit who does the work of the Father on the earth want us to know that a well of water springs up into everlasting life in us. This well of water can be of such force and sweetness of His Spirit that three thousand plus souls can be added to any of His present day churches by ministers who operate with the flaming fire of the glory and power of God in us, on us, and serving others through us.

This is the position, possession, power, and glory that God is restoring to the present day church. He wants us to position ourselves for the greater movement of His Spirit in revival on the earth. What Adam lost when he sinned, Christ regained, reconciled, and restored in His death, burial, and resurrection. This was the process of His giving back to the church that which was lost. "For this purpose the Son of God was manifested, that He might destroy the works of the devil" (1 John 3:8b). "And so it is written, the first man Adam was made a living soul; the last Adam was made a quickening spirit" (1 Cor. 15:45).

This same quickening Spirit of Christ makes and develops His church to do the tremendously great exploits of God in saving the multitudes of men by signs and wonders. Had not the apostles and others with them possessed faith, patience, and obedience to our ascended Lord Jesus, they would have missed the promise of the Father to send the Comforter, the blessed Holy Spirit, to them. He, the Spirit of God, "sat upon each of them," preparing and equipping them to establish the great works of the church in Jerusalem. They also set the stage for the gospel to go forth with the Fire of God to the uttermost parts of the earth.

Down through the ages, since the Holy Spirit endowed men and women with fire, God has been seeking men who have endured the test of time, walked faithfully with Him, and shunned evil. "For the eyes of the LORD run to and fro throughout the whole earth, to shew himself strong in the behalf of them whose heart is perfect toward him" (2 Chron. 16:9a). These are those upon whom God's Spirit will descend and ascend to instill the power of God with such depth and magnitude that they will take absolute authority over the works of Satan and trample upon his demons. Here is Jesus' account on the authority that He has given us:

> And the seventy returned again with joy, saying, "Lord, even the devils are subject unto us through thy name." And He said unto them, "I beheld Satan as lightening fall from heaven. Behold, I give unto you power to tread on serpents and scorpions, and over all the power of the enemy: and nothing shall by any means hurt you. Notwithstanding in this rejoice not, that the spirits are subject unto you; but rather rejoice, because your names are written in heaven."
>
> —Luke 10:17–20

In spite of the slow progress that the church of God seems to be making, God is returning to His people their heritage of possessing the land where they proclaim the gospel of Jesus as they tread across our nation and foreign countries. Our Almighty Father is strategically positioning the church to restore to it the spiritual and natural heritage that Adam lost. We shall have a larger portion of the wealth of the wicked to spread the gospel of the kingdom of God and heaven. We shall receive the power of God to bind Satan and his demons and to prevent the spiritual hindrance and procrastination that the forces of hell have caused in the church. We shall loose the power of the Holy Spirit within our churches, our homes, our schools, and our major institutions of society to implement revival over this land. God's people will return to the God of our salvation, and God will save this world as it chooses to accept Him and heal our land. This is the great hope for our country that is experiencing moral decadence and the downfall of its people. God said in His Word:

If my people, which are called by my name, shall humble themselves, and pray, and seek my face, and turn from their wicked ways; then will I hear from heaven, and will forgive their sin, and heal their land. Now mine eyes shall be open, and mine ears attent unto the prayer that is made in this place. For now have I chosen and sanctified this house, that my name may be there for ever: and mine eyes and mine heart shall be there perpetually.

—2 Chronicles 7:14–16

I beseech us that, by the mercies of God, we may seek His face so that the flaming fire will be on us perpetually, the fire of the Holy Spirit on the warrior in warfare for the cause of the gospel.

CHAPTER 3

THE MINISTER'S AREAS OF ANOINTING

And be not drunk with wine, wherein is excess; but be filled
with the Spirit; Speaking to yourselves in psalms and hymns
and spiritual songs, singing and making melody in your heart
to the Lord.

—Ephesians 5:18–19

And when he had called unto him his twelve disciples, he *gave
them* power against unclean spirits, *to cast them out*, and *to heal*
all manner of sickness and all manner of disease.

—Matthew 10:1

"I indeed baptize you with water unto repentance: but he
that cometh after me is mightier than I, whose shoes I am
not worthy to bear: he shall baptize you with the Holy Ghost,
and with fire."

—Matthew 3:11

And when the day of Pentecost was fully come, they were
all with one accord in one place. And suddenly there came a
sound from heaven as of a rushing mighty wind, and it filled
all the house where they were sitting. And there appeared unto
them cloven tongues like as of fire, and it sat upon each of

them. And they were all filled with the Holy Ghost, and began to speak with other tongues, as the Spirit gave them utterance.

—Acts 2:1–4

Jesus, our Savior, stated some very clear verses about our salvation and what should accompany it as evidence of our knowing Him as the Redeemer of our spirits in the Great Commission:

And he said unto them, "Go ye into all the world, and preach the gospel to every creature. He that believeth and is baptized shall be saved; but he that believeth not shall be damned. And these signs shall follow them that believe; In my name shall they cast our devils; they shall speak with new tongues; they shall take up serpents; and if they drink any deadly thing, it shall not hurt them; they shall lay hands on the sick, and they shall recover."

—Mark 16:15–18

One of the major focuses here is on salvation and the signs following those of us who believe on Jesus and accept Him as our Savior and Redeemer. Here is the first of the three stages of the anointing for a child of God before he is a minister of Jesus, our Chief Minister and Shepherd of the Church. Jesus was also *the Greatest Flame of Fire of all of God's Ministers.* The aforementioned verses point to the signs following believers as casting out devils, speaking with new tongues, and laying hands on the sick for their healing. This comes about through our belief in Christ Jesus. These verses give no indication that only called ministers of God are so anointed to do signs or miracles. The major focus is on "them that believe" on Jesus and are saved. Can we conclude then that every saved child of God receives the Holy Spirit, the anointing of God at the initial experience of salvation? Of course we can. These verses clearly say this; and we should let the Word of God be true and every man a liar. Unfortunately, believers have sometimes not recognized the reality of God's endowing them with the Holy Spirit and the anointing when God saved them. (I, too, *was* included among those believers.)

The majority of believers in Jesus go without this tremendous and marvelous power of God within us. Therefore, like the hungry man on the luxurious ship who was unaware, until shortly before docking at his destination, that his fare covered his meals, we do not know what we have in Jesus Christ because the name of Christ means "Anointed One." Since we are unaware of our anointing, we do not know what we can do with what we have.

This book focuses on what we can do with the anointing that Jesus has given to the called-out body of Jesus Christ with the focus on the laity and His ministers, flames of fire. The church of Jesus Christ must know this. John, the Beloved, was certainly aware of the ability of the anointing to teach us to know all things that are necessary about life and godliness. He said, "But ye have an unction from the Holy One, and ye know all things" (1 John 2:20). Later in the same chapter he says, "But the anointing which ye have received of him abideth in you, and *ye need not that* any man teach you: but as the same anointing teacheth you of all things, and is truth, and is no lie, and even as it hath taught you, ye shall abide in him" (1 John 2:27). The first stage of our anointing occurs when we accept Jesus the Christ (the Anointed One) as our Savior. This happens before God calls us as ministers of any fivefold ministry. Every child of God has the anointing of God's Spirit whether or not he is knowledgeable of this grand and great possession of the Holy Unction.

The initial experience of receiving Jesus as Savior and Lord with the Holy Spirit of God entering our heart (spirit) is the seedbed for the anointing of God to begin His work in us as we yield ourselves to Him. Paul admonishes us in Romans 12:1–2:

> I beseech you, therefore, brethren, by the mercies of God, that ye present your bodies a living sacrifice, holy, accept- able unto God, which is your reasonable service. And be not conformed to this world; but be ye transformed by the

renewing of your mind, that ye may prove what is that good,
and acceptable, and perfect will of God.

As we yield ourselves as sacrifices to Him in the similitude of
Jesus' death for us, we die to our personal gratifications of the
flesh. As we present ourselves to God as tabernacles of His Holy
Spirit, God honors and favors that and increases His anointing in
and on us and on our lives. This sanctification becomes acceptable
to God. The anointing of God's Holy Spirit is now increasing in us
as we realize we are in this world yet not of this world, but citizens
of a greater kingdom, God's Kingdom. As we refuse to become
conformed to this world's custom of living in the corruption of
the flesh and its desires, we become transformed by renewing
our minds through the inner working of the Word of God in
our hearts and lives. This puts us into a position wherein God
proves by the inner working of His Spirit in our spirit what is His
good, acceptable, perfect will. Even at this point, the anointing,
the power of the Living God in us, is still developing us into the
vessels He wants us to be.

Obedience to God is the basis for our blessings and success. Yet
we take many of His directives as though they were suggestions.
God's directives are commands or imperatives for us. Obedient
people walk by faith according to His commandments in the full
counsel of God. An obedient people are faithful to Him because
they love Him and do His commandments.

Why does God give commandments? He is the Commander
in Chief of His armed forces. God prepares His people for war.
There are many battles for us to win. If we are to win lawfully, as
He plans for us to do, we must realize that it's not by might nor
by our power that we win, but by His Spirit. This realization is
a great milestone and position in Christ. We must grow in the
anointing of His Spirit after our initial salvation in the Lord.
For this position is that of a soldier having recently enlisted in
the Lord's armed forces. Yet it is a position of becoming tough
in the Lord, for we pay a price to become more highly anointed

by God as a soldier of Jesus. Toughness, you say? Yes! Toughness. Paul told Timothy:

> Thou therefore endure hardness, as a good soldier of Jesus Christ. No man that warreth entangleth himself with the affairs of this life; that he may please him who hath chosen him to be a soldier. And if a man also strive for masteries, yet is he not crowned, except he strive lawfully. The husbandman that laboureth must be first partaker of the fruits.
>
> —2 Timothy 2:3–6

Those of us who are God's soldiers are expected to train other soldiers in toughness for God. How shall we do this if we have not first had our experiences of hardness as partakers of the fruits? In order to plant or share these fruits with others, our experiences must cause us to become possessors of the fruits we must share.

We must pay the price for the anointing, especially for the increased anointing of God's Spirit. Many an enlisted person in military service might have fared better during his tour of duty if he had counted the cost for each higher level or promotion. Likewise, many a child of God would fare better in forging a closer fellowship with Christ Jesus if he or she first understood that the cost is great. We must endure tough times. The soldier of Christ must know that persecution is an occupational hazard, but knowing Jesus, God the Father, and the Holy Spirit as Keeper and Comforter insuring God's love and care, is more than worth it all. With each promotion, there is a price for discipleship.

According to Luke, one day there was a great crowd with Jesus:

> And there went great multitudes with him: and he turned, and said unto them. "If *any man* come to me, and hate not his father, and mother, and wife, and children, and brethren, and sisters, yea, and his own life also, he cannot be my disciple. And *whosoever doth not* bear his cross, and come after me, cannot be my disciple. For which of you, intending to build a tower, sitteth not down *first*, and counteth the cost, whether he have sufficient to finish it? Lest haply, after he hath laid the foundation, and is not able to finish it, all that behold it begin

43

to mock him, Saying, 'This man began to build, and was not able to finish.' Or what king, going to make war against another king, sitteth not down first, and consulteth whether he be able with ten thousand to meet him that cometh against him with twenty thousand? Or else while the other is a great way off, he sendeth an ambassage, and desireth conditions of peace. So likewise, whosoever he be of you that forsaketh not all that he hath, cannot be my disciple."

—Luke 14:25–33

The price we pay is none other than having Jesus as the first priority in the entirety of our lives with a view to all important persons and things prioritized in right order. Ultimately, Jesus said, "Whosoever doth not bear his cross, and come after me, cannot be my disciple."

We must bear the cross that God gives us and follow Him as we seek to realize our vision. Therein is the guidance and leading of the wise Spirit of God. This, we must share with new converts to the Lord who want to do great exploits for God and be greatly used by Him. We must prepare them for the toughness, the hardness, and the challenges of discipleship and enlistment in the greatest military force on earth, God's armed forces of the Holy Spirit.

Well, you might say, "You've really emphasized experiencing hardness in order to be a good soldier of God." Yes, I have, but not nearly enough. I really can't emphasize this area sufficiently. Because God really wants to trust us with His anointing to do great exploits for Him. Yet He demands of Himself careful and wise selection of those whom He will trust with the glory, the greater measure of His Holy Spirit's power. He bases that decision on our character, our reliability, our fellowship, our intimacy, and our faithfulness to Him as well as our previous work record of carrying out our assignments.

I cite one of my experiences in the Air Force to exemplify the point of a greater measure of anointing. I overheard two supervisors talking about selecting a person to complete a task because the base commander was going to inspect our work section. The supervisors mentioned several people for the job, but then one of them said, "If Cromwell does it, we'll get more done." I got the assignment, and I understood the level of trust that they had in me. My co-workers and I did the assignment to the best of our ability—with excellence. Now, would it not be great for any one of God's ministers, God's flames of fire, to overhear God our Father, Jesus our Savior, and the Holy Spirit in conversation about assigning us a greater vision of tremendous responsibility? How much more diligent might we be if we knew that God selected us because of our faithfulness in previous work assignments? We would really put our shoulders to the plow to fulfill and finish the course in the spirit of excellence. Sometimes when we are unwilling to do our best, we miss the greater blessings of God by doing things our way rather than God's way.

King Saul of Israel was a good example of missing the greater blessing. The Bible says:

> And he tarried *seven days*, according to the set time that Samuel had appointed: but Samuel came not to Gilgal; and the people were scattered from him. And Saul said, "Bring hither a burnt offering to me, and peace offerings." And he offered the burnt offering. And it came to pass, that as soon as he had made an end of offering the burnt offering, behold, Samuel came; and Saul went out to meet him, that he might salute him. And Samuel said, "What hast thou done?" And Saul said, "Because I saw that the people were scattered from me, and that thou camest not within the days appointed, and that the Philistines gathered themselves together at Mishmash; therefore said I, the Philistines will come down now upon me at Gilgal, I have not made supplication unto the LORD: I forced myself therefore, and offered a burnt offering." And Samuel said to Saul, "Thou hast done foolishly: Thou hast not kept the commandment of the LORD thy God, which he commanded thee: for now would the LORD have established thy kingdom upon Israel forever. But now thy kingdom shall not continue: the LORD hath

sought him a man after his own heart, and the Lord hath commanded him to be captain over his people, because thou hast not kept that which the Lord commanded thee."

—1 Samuel 13:8–14

It is wrong to do things according to our feelings and sight. It is not faith that causes us to act out of fear. Fear is the opposite of faith. Fear is one of the greatest tools of Satan. Satan knows that the sinner fears accepting Jesus as Lord and Savior because he thinks that he will not find pleasure in Christ. If he discovers pleasure in Jesus, he also finds fulfillment of spirit and soul in Christ, the Anointed One.

Saul feared the Philistines, Satan's earthly army, and his own people. The Israelite soldiers deserted. Saul took matters into his own hands, and forfeited the establishment of his kingdom forever. Saul's impatience and disobedience caused him to *miss God's blessings and favor*. From Saul, we can learn the fruit of patience with God and the disappointment that impatience brings into our lives. Patience increases our faith in God and the Holy Spirit for accomplishing the perfect will of God.

We have to hear the voice of God with sensitivity to His Spirit: "Behold, to obey is better than sacrifice, and to hearken than the fat of rams" (1 Sam. 15:22b). It is important that we do not miss the glory of His increased anointing for our position and office of ministry because of rebellion. "For rebellion is as the sin of witchcraft, and stubbornness is as iniquity and idolatry. Because thou hast rejected the word of the LORD, he hath also rejected thee from being king" (1 Sam. 15:23). Let us never be guilty of rejecting God's Word. For when we reject His Word, He passes His blessings on to someone who is faithfully seeking His Face and being obedient to Him as Father.

Obedience to God and toughness lead to the second major stage, the infilling of the Holy Spirit. This second stage overlaps the first. Therefore, it is no easy task to separate one stage from the other; however, I shall write it as the Holy Ghost reveals it to me. The infilling of the Holy Ghost is, first of all, demanded by God:

> And be not drunk with wine, wherein is excess; but be filled with the Spirit. Speaking to yourselves in psalms and hymns and spiritual songs, singing and making melody in your heart to the Lord; Giving thanks always for all things unto God and the Father in the name of our Lord Jesus Christ; Submitting yourselves one to another in the fear of God.
>
> —Ephesians 5:18–21

Let us focus on the verb "*be*" in Ephesians 5:18, "And *be* not drunk with wine, wherein is excess; but *be* filled with the Spirit." The first *be* means "to remain or continue." So "be not drunk with wine" means to remain or to continue in sobriety. Moreover, the second clause of that sentence says to remain or continue to be filled with the Spirit of God. Be filled with the Spirit of God. Be filled with God, for the Spirit of God is God Himself. God is the Holy Spirit. God wants to fill us with His Spirit continuously, and He wants us to *remain* filled with Him.

How can we work with God to make this a reality in our lives? We must observe the directive in verse 19: "Speaking to yourselves in psalms and hymns and spiritual songs, singing and making melody in your heart to the Lord." The Hebrews sometimes sang psalms in worshipping God. We can do the same, and we can repeat these in our heart for comfort, joy, and cheer. The Holy Spirit sanctions this method to encourage us individually and corporately in praise and worship. We can also sing hymns and songs in the Spirit of God in our hearts. Spirituals, songs of the Lord as the Spirit of God leads in flowing with His Spirit, often reveal knowledge. They, too, mean praise and worship to God as we focus on Him and not ourselves. As we sing, we make melody, spiritual sounds that are pleasing to the Lord, and we invite His Spirit into our lives. In essence, our efforts determine if God's Spirit continuously refills us.

"Giving thanks always for all things unto God and the Father in the name of our Lord Jesus Christ," cited in Ephesians 5:20, cannot be ignored or overlooked, for this verse is important to God and to us. It demands the co-relevance of Romans 8:28,

"And we know that all things work together for good to them that love God, to them who are the called according to his purpose." Giving thanks for all things does not mean that we are thankful for the bad things in our lives. But these two verses can help us to understand that we can thank God and draw strength from Him in spite of our circumstances because of our faith in Him, the All Powerful and Mighty Father, who works all things out for our good according to His plan for us.

Often times, in order for the majority of Christians to recognize and come into the anointing of God, it is necessary for God to tap that latent Holy Spirit within their spirits by the laying on of hands. The baptism of the Holy Spirit, evidenced by speaking in tongues, may occur at this time. Our Holy God and Father wants us to experience His divine power; He wants to give us all things that pertain to life and godliness. He desires to do this through knowledge of Him who has called us to His glory and power. God desires believers to experience the fullness of His glory and the exceeding greatness of His power according to the working of His mighty power. Therefore, this third stage of the Anointing is required if we are to become fully equipped to carry out spiritual-military assignments in this physical and natural life for the General (God) above all generals of the heaven and earth.

The fourth stage of the fire of God's anointing requires more space than could be allowed in this chapter. Herein it is the central point of where God is presently leading His church in these last days before the fullness of time. We are to experience the greatest anointing, the glory and dominion in our being to be the channels of Holy Spirit's anointing. If we are to know the greatest anointing by the fire of the Holy Spirit, we must receive it from an intimate fellowship with God. As I researched the miraculous works of God through men of faith in the Bible, the greatest were those who had the closest walks with God. For example, the Word says, "And the *Lord spake unto Moses face to face*, as a man speaketh unto his friend. And he turned again into the camp: but his servant Joshua, the son of Nun, a young man, departed not out of the tabernacle" (Exod. 33:11). . . . "And he said, 'My presence shall go with thee, and I will give thee rest'" (Exod. 33:14).

Moses talking with God face to face is parallel with Jesus communicating with God face to face. God would do more miraculous works through Jesus His only Begotten Son than He did through Moses. It is noteworthy that we observe the pattern of Jesus the Christ, the Anointed One, in His *quality, private times* with God.

> And straightway Jesus constrained his disciples to get into a ship, and go before him unto the other side, while he sent the multitudes away. And when he had sent the multitudes away, he went up into the mountain apart to pray. And when the evening was come, he was there alone.
>
> —Matthew 14:22–23

"And when he was alone, they that were about him with the twelve asked of him the parable. And he said unto them, 'Unto you is given to know the mystery of the kingdom of God; but *unto them* that are without, all these things are done in parables.'" (Mark 4:10–11)

> And straightway he constrained his disciples to get into the ship, and to go to the other side before unto Bethsaida, while he sent away the people. And when he had sent them away, he departed into a mountain to pray. And when even was come, the ship was in the midst of the sea, and he alone on the land.
>
> —Mark 6:45–47

This was the secret of the Master Jesus' power with God and His conquests over Satan and man. He prayed alone early in the morning or sometimes during the day and night. The praying gave Him the power of the Holy Spirit to overcome circumstances, trials, temptations, or weapons that Satan threw at Him. By prayer, He received the Holy Spirit. "Now when all the people were baptized, it came to pass, that Jesus also being baptized, and *praying*, the heaven was opened, And the Holy Ghost descended in a bodily shape *like a dove* upon him, and a voice came from heaven, which said, 'Thou art *My Beloved Son*; in thee I am well pleased'" (Luke 3:21–22).

Jesus knew the importance of communicating and being intimate with God, the Father. This is still a prerequisite and continuous requirement to receive a fresh anointing of the Holy Spirit. Jesus was God in flesh, yet He was very human like you and me. The human side of Him needed the glory of God to do the works that He did. The works were supernaturally miraculous. No other man could have fed five thousand or more people with just five loaves of bread and two fishes. No one else could still a storm that threatened His life and the disciples in a boat on a tempestuous sea. His calling was to do the works that no other man had done before Him. Yet, He said to those disciples who would become the first apostles of the beginning of the New Testament Church, "Verily, Verily, I say unto you, *He that believeth* on me, the works that I do shall he do also; and greater works than these shall he do; because I go unto my Father" (John 14:12).

Here Jesus was sowing the seeds of miraculous, supernatural works of God in them to spread the Word of God and to do the divine work of God in different parts of the earth. God's Word is in us, His adopted children. God, Jesus, and the Holy Spirit have broken the ground of our hearts, thrown out the stones, fertilized and watered our hearts with God's Word to do the will of God on the earth. Our commission is to carry forth and spread the Word of God with preaching and teaching to the ends of the earth. God anointed us for this purpose. Jesus admonished His disciples, "Go ye therefore, and teach all nations, baptizing them in the name of the Father, and of the Son, and of the Holy Ghost: teaching them to observe all things whatsoever I have commanded you: and, lo, I am with you always, even unto the end of the world. Amen" (Matt. 28:19–20). Observe with me the purpose of the spreading of the Word and doing the works.

Jesus made a very profound yet simple statement in John 14:11: "Believe me that I am in the Father, and the Father in me: or else believe me for the very works' sake."

God designed the Word and the works to bring men of all races, creeds, religions, and ethnicities to Jesus. From the age of Jesus to the present day, men have believed in the works of God, yet they have missed the purpose of the works: "Believe Me for the works' sake." It is obvious that the Supreme God separated the firmament of the sky and the clouds from the waters on earth. Man benefits from both, yet he still rejects Christ by not believing in and accepting Him. Too many men and women who are legally married do not accept or trust their mates. Unfortunately, men do the same with Jesus. During distressing times, man calls on Jesus for help, rescue, and deliverance yet refuses to believe in the Anointed One for salvation. This is to their destruction. It would seem obvious that, if Jesus can rescue and deliver, He can also save. This is why Jesus said:

> "Therefore speak I to them in parables: *because* they seeing see not; and hearing they hear not, neither do they understand. And in them is fulfilled the prophecy of Esaias, which saith, 'By hearing ye shall hear, and shall not understand; and seeing ye shall see, and shall not perceive: for this people's heart is waxed gross, and their ears are dull of hearing, and their eyes they have closed; lest at any time they should see with their eyes and hear with their ears, and should understand with their heart, and should be converted, and I should heal them.'"
> —Matthew 13:13–16

The main purpose of the Word and the works was for men to believe in Jesus, but if men did not believe in Him, then they should believe in Him for the works' sake, the signs or miracles He performed. Consequently, they would be saved and receive eternal life.

Nevertheless, Jesus' statements were clear. He was human, yet He was the Son of God, fully ministering the gifts of the Holy Ghost in service to other people. The Scriptures show that

Jesus exemplified selflessness concerning position, prestige, and power. We, also, must be careful for these are pitfalls toward a consequential ineffectiveness in ministry. The effect of the pitfalls may not appear right away, but they are insidious.

A clear example of the three of these in action was King David, anointed by God as king of Israel, a successful warrior king whose soldiers were at war while he stayed home on the throne ruling his kingdom. One day David fell into the pitfall of power after he rose from his bed and walked upon the roof of his house. He saw a beautiful woman, Bathsheba, bathing. David sent for her. She came into his house and lay with him. She was another man's wife, but that did not stop David. When she informed him of her pregnancy, David sought to cover up his sin, his error in judgment.

David's sin was a misuse and abuse of his power, prestige, and position as king of Israel. He further complicated matters in his desire to avoid the embarrassment of the consequences of his actions. To keep himself and his kingdom from the loss of prestige and status among the other kingdoms, David decided to arrange for Bathsheba's husband to die in battle. His actions, in a moment of weakness, opened the door of attack from other kingdoms and set the stage for a damaged reputation. A man's reputation is worth more than silver or gold, and it adds stability to his position. David's actions created instability within the territory he ruled. The more stable God's ministers are in self-confidence, reputation, and character, the greater God can use them as firebrands in service. The more pure the vessel or God's minister is, the more God can use him as His instrument in service to His people.

Jesus, a pure vessel, answered Mary and Martha's call to come to see about Lazarus, His near-death friend. Lazarus, however, died before Jesus arrived, and Jesus went to the grave. After weeping, He asked the men to remove the stone from the grave. Observe His method under the use of the anointing in John 11:39a, 41–44:

Jesus said, "Take ye away the stone." . . . . Then they took away the stone from the place where the dead was laid. And Jesus lifted up his eyes, and said, "Father I thank thee that thou has heard me. And I knew that thou hearest me always: but because of the people which stand by I said it, that they may believe that thou hast sent me." And when he thus had spoken, he cried with a loud voice, "Lazarus, come forth." And *he that was dead came forth*, bound hand and foot with graveclothes: and his face was bound about with a napkin. *Jesus saith* unto them, "Loose him, and let him go."

Several issues in this passage are worthy of discussion. First, Jesus was confident that God would work through Him as a yielded vessel to God's Spirit. Listen to what He does as a challenge to His faith in God: He told the men, "Take ye away the stone." There was no real use or value to remove the gravestone, unless something significant, far reaching through the ages, was going to occur. However, with faith in God and Himself that God would move to God's glory, He acted against the public's perception of death and decay. He acted radically in public where His reputation, had He failed, would have been damaged. Who would want to open a grave and view a body four days after it was buried? Jesus knew, however, that He would not fail. He knew that Lazarus would come forth from the grave alive.

We must *understand* that *faith in God increases* and *improves our self-confidence*. Paul said in Philippians 4:13, "I can do all things through Christ which strengtheneth me." In today's words, Paul was saying, "My strength is not of me as the source, but it comes from Christ Himself. Because my strength comes from Christ, I can courageously and boldly say, 'I can do all things through Christ's strength in me.' I can say this with faith in God. I can say this with faith in myself that God will work through me because my real strength in the anointing of Jesus Christ is not of myself, but it is in Christ, the hope of glory. Therefore, I boldly proclaim faith in God and myself that Christ works in me and through me. I have this faith. I have this confidence." Oh, how blessed we would be if we believed that what is impossible for us to be or do in the ministry is possible with Christ, the hope of glory, the *Shekinah* glory of God in us! A minister as a flame of fire is of God. He is the *Flame; He is the Fire.*

Secondly, Jesus prayed under the anointing. Therefore, mighty things of God happened. When we pray under the anointing of Christ, the mighty movement of the Spirit occurs. Unique events happen in the realm of the earth. God answers our prayers. We experience peace of mind and release from yokes. God removes burdens and establishes His peace. We experience a higher than usual level of relationship with God. We experience the joy of the Lord. Consequently, we shout praises, and we worship God for who He is and not for what He has done, is doing, or for what He is going to do for us. Herein is the true test of our love for God. Do we love and worship just because He first loved us and died for us, or do we worship Him just because He is God? Do we love Him because of His blessings, gifts, and favor toward us or do we love Him unconditionally as He loves us unconditionally?

Jesus prayed under the anointing and, through the Spirit of God, He received answers to His prayers. He invoked the resurrection power of the Holy Spirit upon Lazarus' dead body, and Lazarus came forth alive because Jesus *prayed in the will of God. Jesus was confident* in His knowledge of His Father's promises: "And this is the confidence that we have in him, that, if we ask any thing according to his will, he heareth us. And if we know that he hear us, whatsoever we ask, we know that we have the petitions that we desired of him" (1 John 5:14–15). Jesus knew the secret of having His prayers answered. The *secret* was *praying according to God's will.* He lived according to the Word of God. He prayed according to God's will. He prayed the Word of God. If we want answered prayers, we too must pray according to His Word. When we pray according to God's Word, He will answer our prayers because *God's Word contains His will. It expresses the very will of God* as *it is in His mind.*

Many of us have unanswered prayers because we are unaware that the Word of God expresses His mind, just as our word expresses our minds. God's Word contains His heartfelt expressions. In His Word, He is being intimate with us. Therefore, *He wants to call us "friends" and not "servants." He wants to raise us to a higher level of intimacy with Him.* "Henceforth I call you not servants; for the servant knoweth not what his lord doeth: but I have called you friends; for all things that I have heard of my Father I have made known unto you" (John 15:15).

Thirdly, Jesus thanked God for hearing and answering His prayer. He was calling those things that were not as though they already existed. In the eye of the Spirit, He already saw Lazarus alive. In our eye of the Spirit, we too must see our prayers answered, our vision coming forth. It must be a walk by faith and not natural sight. We, too, must call those things into existence that are not as though they already existed here in the earth. Jesus expressed His gratitude to God for answering His prayer. Thanking God is part of our praising Him. The curses came upon the Israelites because they refused to live according to God's will and with joyful and glad hearts.

> Moreover all these curses shall come upon thee, and shall pursue thee, and overtake thee, till thou be destroyed; because thou hearkenedst not unto the voice of the LORD thy God, to keep his commandments and his statues which he commanded thee. And they shall be upon thee for a sign and for a wonder, and upon thy seed for ever. Because thou servedst not the LORD thy God with joyfulness, and with gladness of heart, for the abundance of all things.
> —Deuteronomy 28:45–47

A very important part of getting our prayers answered is to thank, praise, and worship God in gladness and joyfulness for prayers He has answered and blessings He has bestowed upon us.

The resurrection power of the anointing was also applied to Lazarus' return from the dead. Paul cites this power in Philippians 3:10: "*That I may know him,* and the power of his resurrection, and the fellowship of his sufferings, being made conformable unto his death." Paul desired a resurrection from sin (death) into spiritual life with Christ. He desired also to suffer for Christ in order to press toward the mark for the prize of the high calling of God in Christ Jesus. However, the power of the resurrection of Jesus is also the power of the anointing. It was the anointed power of God in Jesus that raised the Messiah, *The Anointed One,* from the dead. Christ said in John 10:17–18, "Therefore doth my Father love me, because I lay down my life, that I might take it again. No man taketh it from me, but *I lay it down of myself.* I have power to lay it down, I have power to take it again. This commandment have I received of my Father."

When Jesus raised the dead, it was the power of the anointing to destroy the yoke of death. When He turned water into wine, it was the power of the Resurrection to transform one substance into something different and new, such as a *newness* of life. Lazarus' resurrection was a transformation from death into a new life. When Jesus walked on water, it was bringing something into being that was dead to the mind and heart of man. It was to bring into the natural life a radical change in man's heart, mind, and life. When Jesus restored sight to the blind, it was bringing sight—something new—into a body part that was dead. When Jesus healed the leprous skin of lepers, it was bringing new skin into life for them. These are examples of the power of the Resurrection! Therefore, as Jesus was radical in His beliefs/faith, motivations, and actions, He seeks to make us radical. His purpose is to develop us as flaming fires, radical leaders in Him and for Him.

CHAPTER 4

THE FLAMING FIRE MINISTER, A RADICAL LEADER FOR GOD

God's highly anointed ministers whom He would promote to different dimensions are developed and guided by the Holy Spirit, who leads them to a stage of radicalism. God's firebrands do not become radical in the negative sense of the word, but in the positive, to bring about the radical change of salvation, growth, development, and prosperity in the lives of others.

When a person receives Jesus as Lord and Savior, something different occurs in that person's heart and life. This is especially observable if the new convert to the Lord studies, meditates, and continuously applies the Word of God to his life. He lives for Christ; he fleshes out the divine Word in his life. We are apt to say that Tom is different. He no longer indulges in alcoholic beverages; the partying in the secular sense of the word ceases. He abruptly stops speaking vulgarities and obscenities. He no longer womanizes, but he is faithful to one woman. What has happened?

Jesus Christ's saving power has caused a radical change in his life. Is this bad? No, it is good. Is this evil? No, it is righteous. Is it bad for Tom? No! His rebirth is the best and greatest thing since his day of natural birth. He has experienced a spiritual birth. We recall that Jesus told Nicodemus that he must be born again. Jesus was expressing the radical change that Rabbi Nicodemus needed to experience. There are many Nicodemuses in the world who need the radical change of salvation, the inner working of the Word of God, and the Holy Spirit in their lives. All of us need the radical change that God desires to continuously develop in our lives.

Another example might involve a former drug lord who suddenly ceases to sell drugs. He still goes to the same areas where he obtained great sums of money by ruining the lives of any person who partook in his evil trade. Now, however, he pushes Jesus Christ to other pushers who knew him well, and he leads them to his Lord and Savior. What has happened? What or who brought about this tremendous and extreme change in his life? The Radical Jesus caused the lifestyle change. The former drug pusher is so glad to know Jesus as his Savior from darkness and evil that he is fulfilled and glad—joyful, in fact—to risk his life among current pushers to lead them to his miraculous Jesus Christ. Is this radical? Yes, but look at the goodness of the Lord in radicalism in the positive sense of the word. Is this a departure from the norm of the world and traditionalism of secularism? Yes, a thousand times, yes!

According to Webster's Dictionary, *radical* is "1. Of or from the root or roots, going to the foundation or source of something; fundamental; basic (a radical principle), (b) extreme; thorough (a radical change in one's life), 2. (a) favoring basic change in the social or economic structure!" If we analyze this definition of *radical*, first, we would not be on the earth as human beings if God had not created an earth that, in its former state was without form and void, a wasteful and empty place. Secondly, God did something else that was also extreme and far from the norm of things by creating a man, Adam, from the dust of the ground and breathing into him the breath of life. All of the creative acts of God, including the first operation on man, the removal of one of his ribs to create Eve, were radical; yet they were rooted in God, the source and the most basic fundamental of man's life. If it were not for a radical, creative God, we would not be here. If it were not for the radical death, resurrection, and ascension of Jesus, spiritually blind men, who are lost in sin, would not receive the gift of salvation. If for no other reason, we should praise God, the Creator and our Spiritual Father for His creative acts. Praise and glory be to Jesus for the radical miraculous salvation He has given to us. I am thankful to God for salvation, for radicalism, for the seal of His Spirit, and the holy power of the anointing.

God is radical. Jesus is radical. The Holy Spirit is radical. The anointing is radical in what it does in resurrection power. And if we, Christ's ministers, are to bring about a radical change to the present social and economic structure in society that is sustaining and lasting, we too, must be radical in how we allow the Lord Jesus to use us by being sensitive to His Holy Spirit to lead us.

Now, let us look again at this great positive word *radical,* which means "from the root or roots, going to the foundation or source of something." When Jesus turned the water into wine at the wedding feast, this was basic yet radical, because it referred men at the event to God, the source who created the liquid water from which Jesus made the wine. Grapes have no liquid without the basic root source of water. When Jesus fed more than five thousand people, He referred them to God, the source of the bread and the fishes of the sea.

When Jesus developed a healing salve of spit and dirt and applied it to the blind man's eyelids, He pointed men's hearts to God, the foundation of life who can bring sight from blindness, dispelling the darkness. When Jesus raised Lazarus from the grave to newness of natural, physical life, again He was leading man's heart to the power of the source of life, His Father, and the power of the anointing Holy Spirit. When Jesus stilled the deadly, devastating storm that threatened to take the lives of His disciples, He caused men to question who He was. Again, He was leading men to believe in the creative power of God over the elements of nature that God created—no God, no elements of nature; God, yes, elements of nature, yes.

When Jesus died on Golgotha Hill, the Place of the Skull, and by His own power was resurrected in the prophesized time, His resurrection indicated that Father God had given Him power over death and any named and appointed place of unfair human execution. Therefore, Jesus provides the basics, the rooting and source of God in salvation. Our God is the source of life, the power over death, and the radical change of salvation.

Even the gifts of the Holy Spirit are fundamental or radical. According to our churches and ministers, many of our schools of higher learning and traditional seminaries teach about the radical Spirit of God. In traditional seminary doctrine, the gifts of the Holy Spirit are recognized by these schools as operative during the founding of the New Testament church in the book of Acts but are not operative in today's New Testament church. The usual doctrine is that, when the apostles such as Peter, Paul, and John the Revelator died, so did the gifts of the Holy Spirit, as well as the fivefold office of pastor, prophet, evangelist, teacher, and apostle. Preaching and teaching differently from this traditional seminary point of view is radical.

The liberal, conservative, and modernistic minister and church as well as those who support the inerrancy of the Bible have a problem with applying radicalism to teaching and preaching. The implication is that we believe the Word of God with limitations. We limit our acceptance to the Scriptures or scriptural passages that please or that just change our style of living up to a certain point. The Scriptures we readily accept are those that sound good and/or that can be used to our benefit, but we refuse the whole of the divine Word because it would challenge us in all areas of Christian lifestyle. We are partial Scripture believers.

This applies to our belief that God so loved the world that He gave His only Begotten Son that whosoever believes in Him should not perish but have everlasting life. This we believe and accept. We have difficulty, however, and are reluctant to believe the quote attributed to God in Malachi 3:6a—"For I am the LORD, I change not . . ." Yet, this same God who through the gifts of the

Holy Jesus Christ and the apostles wrought signs and wonders in the early New Testament church changes not in our day. This same Holy God who through the gifts of the Holy Spirit saved, healed, and wrought miracles, still operates these gifts through the anointing in men and women today. Men and women who God anoints with the Holy Spirit and endues with His power can do the works of God on the earth. These individuals, chosen to perform in certain offices of ministry with different functions within the body of Christ, spread the gospel of Christ to the ends of the earth. God commissions us, through the Holy Spirit, to implement the Great Commission. Jesus intercedes for us in prayer so that each of us, wholeheartedly, with sensitivity to the guidance and leading of the Holy Spirit, will completely fulfill our calling.

To fulfill the calling to ministry of any kind, we are purposed by God to lead people to Jesus Christ from all walks of life. How are we to do this as the firebrands of God? Our preaching the good news of the saving Jesus must be Jesus-led, Jesus-inspired, and Jesus-endued with the Holy Spirit's power and not influenced by the corrupt power of man who would attempt to pressure us to not spread the radical life-changing message of the counsel of God. Our teaching must be established with the power of the Holy Spirit. "Not by might, nor by power, but by my spirit, saith the LORD of hosts" (Zech. 4:6). To prepare others as servants of Christ Jesus, our teaching has to be from a servant's position if others who would enter service of any kind to Christ are themselves to be most effective in their work. Jesus established this position for us in Mark 10:35–45:

> And James and John, the sons of Zebedee, come unto him, saying, "Master, we would that thou shouldest do for us what-soever we shall desire." And he said unto them, "What would ye that I should do for you?" They said unto him, "Grant unto us that we may sit, one on thy right hand, and the other on thy left hand, in thy glory." But Jesus said unto them, "Ye know not what ye ask: Can ye drink of the cup that I drink of? And

be baptized with the baptism that I am baptized with?" And they said unto him, "We can." And Jesus said unto them, "Ye shall indeed drink of that cup that I drink of; and with the baptism that I am baptized withal shall ye be baptized: But to sit on my right hand and on my left hand is not mine to give; but it shall be given to them for whom it is prepared." And when the ten heard it, they began to be much displeased with James and John. But Jesus called them to him, and saith unto them, "Ye know that they which are accounted to rule over the Gentiles exercise lordship over them; and their great ones exercise authority upon them. But so shall it not be among you: but whosoever will be great among you, shall be your minister: and whosoever of you will be the chiefest, shall be servant of all. For even the Son of man came not to be ministered unto, but to minister, and to give His life a ransom for many."

This is our position of servant. Even as the greatest among our fellow ministers, we are still servants of Christ. According to Jesus, we are still servants to each other, no matter our status in the ministry or walk of life. The playing ground is level at the Cross. The playing ground is level at the feet of the Jesus and in God's echelon of authority.

Whether our ministries are greater or lesser than others, we are positioned as servants to each other and to God. Jesus said, "But he that is greatest among you shall be your servant. And whosoever shall exalt himself shall be abased; and he that shall humble himself shall be exalted" (Matt. 23:11–12). It stands to reason then that God will, by the anointing, exalt the humble spirited minister. He can also humble the proud anointed minister. God promotes whom He will; He demotes whom he chooses. It is up to us. The ball is in our court to remain where we are, to rise to the next dimension, or to descend to a lower dimension. "For promotion cometh neither *from* the east, nor *from* the west, *nor from* the south. But God is the judge: He *putteth* down one, and *setteth* up another" (Ps. 75:6–7). Promotion is of God, the Lord.

The principle of servant, from the lowest to the highest, from the greatest minister to the least, is a very radical doctrine among the children of men. However, this inward character of Jesus makes Him the world's greatest *positive* radical. If we really understood His lifestyle and principles for what they are, we would realize that God, Jesus, and the Holy Spirit require us to be radical like Jesus in our living and service to others.

We talk about being Christlike, but we refuse to study Christ's life and to meditate on what His life means for us and for our actions. To become Christlike demands continuous improvement in our Christian walk. It also means fleshing out the Word of God by being doers of it and not hearers only. It means ministering the challenges of fiery-hot teaching and preaching to those whom we serve. Being like Christ shows in the way we act, and our integrity supports the gospel that we preach and teach, so that its weight and impact will accomplish God's Great Commission of spreading His Word. Are we ministers to be flaming fires for God without being radical in our positions, attitudes, and style of living? No! Each of the men in God's Hall of Faith was somehow radical.

Consider the men listed in Hebrews 11: Abraham, Abel, Enoch, Noah, Isaac, Jacob, Joseph, Moses, Joshua, Gideon, Barak, Samson, Jephethae, David, and Samuel. John the Baptist, Paul, and the apostles were also inducted into God's Hall of Flame. What are some of the examples of radical acts of faith? Think of Abraham, who God called just as He calls us today. To be obedient, Abraham had to leave his home and kinsmen and to go to a place that he would receive as an inheritance. Abraham obeyed God's call even though he did not know the destination to which God was leading him. God still calls us to journey with Him by faith into unknown areas.

A further study of Abraham's character as a radical for God proves that he believed in the unseen, living God who audibly spoke to him from heaven. God commanded Abraham to do some unusual things, things different from the thinking, position, and attitude of majority thought. Follow these Scriptures with me:

> Now the LORD had said unto Abram, "Get thee out of thy country, and from thy kindred, and from thy father's house, unto a land that I will shew thee: And I will make thee a great nation, and I will bless thee, and make thy name great; and thou shalt be a blessing: And I will bless them that bless thee, and curse him that curseth thee: and in thee shall all families of the earth be blessed." So Abram departed, as the LORD had spoken unto him; and Lot went with him: and Abram was seventy and five years old when he departed out of Haran. And Abram took Sarai his wife, and Lot his brother's son, and all their substance that they had gathered, and the souls that they had gotten in Haran; and they went forth to go into the land of Canaan; and into the land of Canaan they came.
> —Genesis 12:1–5

First, it is obvious that Abraham was a man who was sensitive to the voice and Spirit of God. He heard God's voice, received it in his spirit, and obeyed. This is very important. When we are sensitive to God's Spirit, He may speak audibly to us. He gives directions that affect us personally and that impact the lives of those within our sphere of influence. We should never forget that our choices affect other people. If Abraham had not been obedient to God in leaving familiar surroundings, his father, and his kindred to go to a land that God would show him, the Israelites (Jews) might never have become the great chosen people of God to enrich the nations of the earth during the different eras of mankind.

Israel still affects us today. Out of the nation of Israel, Christ Jesus, our Savior and Lord, was born. Jesus was of the lineage of Abraham. (Just the thought of Abraham being disobedient to God's Spirit can make one shudder in his spirit. Because Jesus was born to die as the propitiation for our sins, to rise from the dead, and to save countless millions of people over the ages, perish the thought of Abraham being anything but obedient.) Abraham's actions were not only radical, but they were far-reaching.

Secondly, Abraham believed God and moved with his family, by faith, from his father's house. This was the most important thing Abraham could have done. Because of his faith and trust in God, Abraham became the father of nations. I would like to differentiate his action from his faith. Please understand me. Both his action and his faith are important. However, his faith in God was the most important element here. God's word so eloquently makes this point, "But without faith it is impossible to please him: for he that cometh to God must believe that he is, and that he is a rewarder of them that diligently seek him" (Heb. 11:6). Abraham heard God's audible voice, did not question God, and knew in his heart that God had spoken His marching orders to him. When he acted on God's Word, he acted by faith. Herein is the difference. He acted because of his faith.

Because Abraham acted by faith, he pleased God, and as the Word says in 1 Samuel 15:22, "To obey is better than sacrifice." If you are willing and obedient, you will eat the good of the land! Now, Abraham could have said to God, "God, you are telling me to disrupt my comfort zone. My family and I have been living very *comfortably* in these familiar surroundings here at Daddy's. Yet, you are telling me to not only to get out of his house but also to leave the country. Why would you require this of me?" Suppose Sarai objects and says, "Man, you must be crazy. I'm quite pleased here at Daddy's. We get along very well. He treats me not as a daughter-in-law, but as a daughter. I'm your wife, Abraham, and I deserve some respect for my wishes and needs, and appreciation also. Why should we have to move?"

Abraham could have said to God, "She's right, you know, God. She is my wife. It appears your demands of me could cause problems for my wife and me for years to come. God, you could cause me great grief with this woman. What you're asking will affect her, too. It will affect both of us for years."

Can you see God not changing His mind? When He, the Commander in Chief of the Spiritual Armed Forces, chooses a person to execute His marching orders, He selects His generals in wisdom, understanding, love, generosity, and guidance. He has promised, "I will instruct thee and teach thee in the way which thou shalt go: I will guide thee with mine eye" (Ps. 32:8). (Thank, God, He had absolutely no verbal or physical protest from Abram. This attested to Abram's heart and his willing obedience to follow God by faith.)

Apparently, Sarai knew that Abram was a man of faith, so she did not protest the disturbance of their comfort zone. Thus Abram, with Sarai, his wife, went out, not knowing where he was going. He was sure, however, that God would lead Him. He was sure that God would take care of His own, those who followed the Omnipresent God wherever He led. Abram was secure in the fact that God would protect them from any unseen dangers and that He would build a shelter around those who sincerely follow Him by faith. Abram believed God's promises.

The world yet waits to see what a man who willingly follows God in obedience can do. The world yet waits to see the power of a Christian who absolutely sells out for God and His plans for him. The world still waits for the powerful influence of the anointing power of God in such a person's life. Such an anointed life will affect our world and do great things for our Jesus when led by the Holy Spirit. I pray, may the Lord let you and me be those persons?

Abram journeyed by faith in a faithful God. Now, God still speaks to ministers and provides direction for our lives. Sometimes, we follow it wholeheartedly, and at other times, halfheartedly. To the extent that we follow God's guidance, our blessings and peace will flow from Him. Obedience to God by faith produces His favor and His peace in our heart and our peace with Him. Obedience to God places peace in our inner man and in our fellow man.

Sometimes we hear God and go through the motions without faith. Our lives are filled with activity but empty of faith. Such frenzied activity, such faithlessness can cause ministers to burn out and develop physical and/or emotional problems. Opposition to or disagreement with God's Word creates problems for those who listen but do not hear or who hear but do not understand. (I pray that our hearts and our actions will prove differently.)

In order for us to be flames of fire for Jesus, we are required to make some radical changes in ourselves and to move from our comfort zones. Those changes depend on where we are with God and what He requires of us. The radical actions that are required of us could be inward changes of the heart or they can be outward changes that are motivated by changes in the spiritual man.

God changes not; yet, He expects and demands changes of us. He wants to move us from our comfort zones into His comfort zone for us. This is a continuing task. Remember Jesus' words to Peter: "And the Lord said, 'Simon, Simon, behold, Satan hath desired to have you, that he may sift you as wheat: But I have prayed for thee, *that thy faith fail not*: and when thou art *converted,* strengthen thy brethren'" (Luke 22:31–32). In essence, Jesus was telling Peter, "You are quite satisfied with your relationship to Me. You think that you are fulfilled, but there is something going on in the spiritual realm, in the heavenlies of which you are not aware. Satan has gone before God and asked to have you, to do with you as he chooses. Satan knows your anger, your tendency to be impulsive. He knows that you speak all too hastily and of your tendency to be physically and verbally aggressive. Satan desires to use these weaknesses in you, for they are open doors to him. Don't misunderstand Me, Peter. You are not all bad, for if you were, you could not be My disciple. There is strength in you, but Satan has asked God if he can sift you as wheat. He wants to use the comfort zone of your weakness, so that God cannot use you in the comfort zone He wants to move you into. Since I know both your weaknesses and strengths, Peter, I have prayed *that thy faith fail not*: and when thou art converted, strengthen thy brethren."

In biblical times, the word *sift* had to do with the threshing of grain. Animals walked or trod on the grain; then, using forks, men threw it into the air so that the wind could carry away the chaff. Satan desired to tread on Peter spiritually, emotionally, mentally, and physically, and then throw him to the wind. He desired to thresh Peter so that the good in him would not be effective in serving God and Jesus, as led by the Holy Spirit, after Jesus' ascension into heaven.

Satan recognized that God could use Peter's strength in founding and establishing the New Testament church; therefore, he focused on one of the potential leaders among Jesus' disciples. This is another indication of our Savior Jesus Christ's sensitivity to God in that He said, as "God speaks, I listen and do as God says." He was aware of God's conversation with Satan about Peter. Satan had asked God's permission to "try" Peter even as he had asked God for permission to inflict physical and mental anguish on Job. The Evil One is again attempting to thwart the purposes of God through those whom He had chosen. Satan actually desired to consume Peter by destroying him. Jesus knew this. Therefore, He said to Peter, "But I have prayed for thee, that *thy faith fail not.*"

Here we need to deal with the second important word in these verses. Jesus said, "And when thou art *converted,* strengthen thy brethren." *Converted* here means returned to repentance and faith. Peter had been converted and served God for three years, but he was complacent and headed for a fall. By turning back to his former relationship to God, he would be stronger than before. After his conversion, Jesus wanted Peter to strengthen his brethren. We know that Peter did exactly that during Pentecost when God converted three thousand souls after his first sermon and an additional five thousand souls joined the church after his second sermon. God wants to move us out of our comfort zone to His comfort zone for us.

God's comfort zone for us is the best zone, for therein is His loving favor and a good reputation. "A good name *is* rather to be chosen than great riches, and loving favour rather than silver or gold" (Prov. 22:1). God's loving favor provides the prosperity we need as God's flames of fire. He who seeks the face of God and His kingdom with his whole heart as well as the righteousness of God by moving from his comfort zone to God's comfort zone will receive what he needs from God—faith and God's grace. He will also find the peace of God that transcends comprehension. Because he pleases God, even his enemies will be at peace with him.

However, in God's comfort zone, we will need to be flexible and available so that we can flow in God's will as He gives it by the Holy Spirit. We shall need to allow ourselves to be available to God's will and to continually follow it. We shall need to allow God to mold, make, and shape us into the vessels He desires. He is the potter; we are the clay. In this process, there could very well be a shaking and a breaking of us in order for the Holy Spirit to use His mighty "instruments" marching into battle with Him as Drum Major.

As we follow and march to the cadence of our Drum Major, God leads us to a position of authority in Him, in the power-of-attorney in Jesus' name. Our authority alone is insufficient to do the mighty works of God. By the authority of God, under His anointing, however, we can do great exploits.

CHAPTER 5

AN AWESOME POSITION: ABSOLUTE AUTHORITY IN GOD

"Behold, I send an Angel before thee, to keep thee in the way, and to bring thee into the place which I have prepared. Beware of him, and obey his voice, provoke him not; for he will not pardon your transgressions: for my name is in him. But if thou shalt indeed obey his voice, and do all that I speak; then I will be an enemy unto thine enemies, and an adversary unto thine adversaries. For mine Angel shall go before thee, and bring thee in unto the Amorites, and the Hittites, and the Perizzites, and the Canaanites, and the Hivites, and the Jebusites: and I will cut them off."

—Exodus 23:20–23

God's gospel ministers must have absolute authority and power over all the works of the Devil. As we see in Exodus 23:20–23, God goes before us in battle and spiritual warfare. Our enemies become His enemies; our adversaries become His adversaries. He fights different people of different beliefs on our behalf. He has one condition: "Obey his (angel's) voice, and do all that I speak" (Exod. 23:22). God has given us the inherent position in Him as sons and daughters of God, of having God our Father to fight on our behalf based on our sensitivity to His Holy Spirit and obedience to what He says to position us. Is it not good to know that, by faith established in us and by obedience to God the Father, God fights some battles alone for us, and He does not want us to be involved in the conflict? He simply asks us to stand and to see the salvation of the Lord's hand on us.

God purposefully gave to the disciples and passed to the church of God, the body of Christ, absolute authority and power over Satan and his demons. Luke 10:19 says, "Behold, I *give* unto you power to tread on serpents and scorpions, and over all the power of the enemy: and nothing shall by any means hurt you." Jesus was saying to us, I give you authority over Satan and his demons. Their power and authority are less than that of men of the church, the body of Christ. With Satan under Jesus' feet, the earth serving as His footstool, and us being members of His body, Satan and his demons are under the authority and power of the church because *we are* the body of Jesus.

Again, our position is over Satan and demons as the head and not the tail and being above only and not beneath. We, the church and its leaders, must recognize our awesome position in the Lord Jesus. We must realize the spiritual power given to us as ministers, flames of fire, to destroy the works of Satan in our churches, our communities, and in our lives. This is the greatest position of power given to men on earth by God.

However, there must be a clarion call to alert the church and an amassing of the forces of God to the battlefield for the Lord. This signal warns of the deception of the greatest Enemy of the church and every Christian alive. This, we must instill into our spirits with diligence. First Peter 5:8–9 says, "Be sober, be vigilant; because your adversary the devil, as a roaring lion, walketh about, seeking whom he may devour: Whom resist steadfast in the faith, knowing that the same afflictions are accomplished in your brethren that are in the world."

The Devil promotes hatred in our hearts rather than love and envy rather than admiration and respect for others. The deception is in the havoc, the tribulation, the circumstances, the suffering, and the temptation to commit various kinds of sin. The deception is in the potential for the roots of bitterness to grow in our hearts, rather than prayer for our closest family members, co-workers, and fellow laborers in the Lord. The deception is in the weakening of us in misguided efforts rather than God-led works.

Satan is, first of all, the great Deceiver; he is the cause of any situation or problem in which we are misled, misguided, or off focus from the Lord Jesus' purpose for our lives. We have to be careful that we are not worn out, burnt out, and fearful because the Devil does everything he can to keep us from ever knowing who we are and understanding our greatest position in Christ, our Savior. If Satan can keep us from experiencing this knowledge of our position in Christ, God, and the Holy Spirit, he can devour or consume us to the point that we are still alive but ineffective for the Lord. We may be alive physically but dead toward the things of God that would make the greatest difference in our lives.

Let us view the great deceiver as he really is. The lion is the alleged king of the jungle. One reason for this allegation is the powerful roar of the lion. The sound is so bone-chilling that one might immediately respond in fear. Remember, however, that the roar of the lion causes the fear. One might not see the lion, but he has heard the roar. The lion has not attacked, but the effect of his awesome sound has instilled in you the fear of an attack. The danger seems real. You heard the sound, this great noise, and it has influenced your emotions.

Satan is like the lion. If he can run us off track and out of God's will with the threat of an attack, why should he waste the time and energy to approach us? He has accomplished his purpose with the ominous sound. We must recognize that Satan uses camouflage to keep us from realizing the deception. Too often the potential or possibility for danger deceives us. But God says in 1 Peter 5:8, "Be sober, be vigilant; because your adversary the devil, *as a roaring lion, walketh about, seeking whom he may devour.*" The Word of God doesn't say that he is a roaring lion, it says "*as a roaring lion.*"

I emphasize "*as*" because "as" is very different from "is." "Is" means real. "As," on the other hand, means it is similar to but not the real thing. The Devil creates temptation or desire as part of his great deception to get us to believe in something that is not genuine, to believe in and to act on something that appears real.

A lie is like that; it deceives, manipulates, and misguides or misdirects our steps from the Lord. We must face the reality of who Satan really is. I know no better reference than Jesus' words in John 8:44: "Ye are of your father the devil, and the lusts of your father ye will do. He was a murderer from the beginning, and abode not in the truth, because there is no truth in him. When he speaketh a lie, he speaketh of his own: for he is a liar, and the father of it." Jesus reveals the great deceiver for whom he is: the father of lies, the father of instigation who preys upon the lusts and fears of men to lead them astray. There he, the great manipulator of mankind, claims his own as their father and leads them into hell by the greatest deception of all. That deception is to scare mankind into believing that right is wrong and that wrong is right. The great deception is to motivate mankind into believing that good is bad and that bad is good. Isaiah 5:20 says it like this: "Woe to them that call evil good, and good evil; that put darkness for light, and light for darkness; that put bitter for sweet, and sweet for bitter!"

When the Christian is intimidated into confusing good for bad or righteousness for evil, Satan has achieved his purpose in the Christian's life without directly or physically attacking the child of God. This is likely the time when yielding to temptation occurs. For if nothing else, one's thoughts and attitude or mindset is evil at this point. Weakness of the carnal nature, the flesh, consequently leads to sin. The thought life is evil, and sin takes its course. The sins of adultery, love of money, and drugs become a part of one's life. The more one is involved in sin of any type, the less guilt one feels, and the more effective sin is in one's life. First Timothy 4:1–2 says it well: "Now the *Spirit speaketh* expressly, *that* in the latter times some shall depart from the faith, *giving heed* to seducing spirits, and doctrines of devils. *Speaking* lies in hypocrisy; having their conscience seared with a hot iron." One's conscience does not convince or convict one to repentance toward Jesus Christ, for sin has too great an influence. For instance, as a teenager in school, my mother taught me how to iron my denim jeans and khaki pants. The method was to spray the pants with starch after dampening them and then to apply the hot iron to the wrinkles by running the iron across the material. This process removed the wrinkles from the pants just as the wrinkles of impact and results toward God are removed by continuous sinning. As ministers of God seeking God's face for His anointing to teach and preach God's Word with the greatest results, we must avoid sin as we would AIDS or the bubonic plague.

I have always appreciated the pastor under whose authority I preached my initial message for warning me to avoid what he indicated as the three major areas that often cause ministers' downfall: women, money, and alcoholic beverages. He also said that, because so many "brethren of the cloth" are involved in these, other ministers have to try to live their reputations down. This wise advice still affects my lifestyle today as a called minister of God delivering the gospel message.

If we are to give our utmost for His Highest, we must be aware that Satan's main attack is on God's called and sent ministers who would lead others into the land of God's promises as His written Word declares. The Devil will do whatever is in his power to prevent us from giving ourselves sacrificially as Romans 12:1–2 admonishes us: "I beseech you therefore, brethren, by the mercies of God, that ye present your bodies a living sacrifice, holy, acceptable unto God, which is your reasonable service. And be not conformed to this world: but be ye transformed by the renewing of your mind, that ye may prove what is that good, and acceptable, and perfect, will of God." This is a major part of our awesome position.

Do we get to this juncture overnight? No. Transformation is a continuous process of growing and maturing in the lord. It is an ongoing task of fellowship, walking daily with the Lord, pulling away from the crowd to spend time with Him. It is doing all we can to stay with the Lord during the best of times and the worst of times. It is studying God's Word continuously. It is an ongoing process of learning to be sensitive to God's Holy Spirit and following Him as He leads and where He leads. To be transformed is to learn to praise and thank God and to seek God's face and righteousness. It is learning to develop an intimate relationship with God so that when the Father says: "Be quiet. I want to talk with you," we are silent, and He reveals Himself as He talks with us in our prayer time. It is walking by faith and not by sight in order to please Him. In this awesome position, we endeavor to please God rather than man. Because the loving Word says: "But without faith it is impossible to please him: for he that cometh to God must believe that he is, and that he is a rewarder of them that diligently seek him" (Heb. 11:6). In *The Living Bible*, Proverbs 20:24 states that the Lord directs our steps, so why should we try to understand everything that happens along the way? In other words, our position is not to analyze everything that God allows to happen in our lives. Even when we do not understand it, we are to follow Him because the Lord orders the steps of a good man.

"When a man's ways please the LORD, he *maketh* even his enemies to be at peace with him" (Prov. 16:7). Does this mean only natural man? No, I would say. God has Satan on a leash, so his power to interfere in our lives is limited. When we please God in the ways of the heart, our attitude, and in our actions, God puts the limits on the Devil's roar and attack in our affairs. Consequently, peace ensues even during the onslaughts of Satan.

Praise God that pleasing Jesus causes our enemies to be at peace with us! Praise Father God that following His leadership as the Leader of leaders as we walk in the Spirit gives us peace. Praise the Holy Spirit because as we bring our behavior, our thoughts, and imagination under the subjection of His Spirit, He gives us a peaceful and sound mind. Praise the Holy Trinity because as we yield our lives to Him, the Godhead, He settles and establishes us even in the midst of spiritual warfare.

We must assure ourselves, however, by being in constant communication with God that we are following God and not our own notions of the flesh. It is true that the way of our fleshly lusts and emotions is not the way of following the Lord. This, too, is a deception of Satan. Satan laughs at us when we are so misled. We must instill this verse in our hearts to protect our anointing: "There is a way that seemeth right unto a man, but the end thereof are the ways of death" (Prov. 16:25). *The Living Bible* makes it plain: "Before every man there lies a wide and pleasant road he thinks is right, but it ends in death." What a stop sign to our own selfish ways, self-centeredness, and narcissism!

Therefore, it is vitally important that we avoid selfishness in seeking power with man and yet to seek the anointing power of God as God's way toward becoming a *firebrand for the Lord*. We have to guard our anointing against self-centeredness as to what our heavenly Father wills to do in our lives. This, too, is major in our awesome position as the potential flames of fire for Him who is a Consuming Fire. In our position, we have to protect our anointing as one of the most precious possessions we shall ever be entrusted with by God. Proverbs 4:23 says: "Keep thy heart with all diligence; *for* out of it are the issues of life." Notice the significance of the word "*keep.*"

In a humble attempt to relate it to our precious anointing, first, "*Keep* thy heart with all diligence." *Heart* in Scripture refers not only to the physical heart but, more importantly, to the spirit of man. Who is in our spirit? Christ Himself is in our spirit. The name *Christ* means "Deliverer of His people from their sins." The Greek word for "Christ" is *Christos*, which means "the Anointed One, the Messiah." In that the Anointed One is Jesus who is in our hearts, it becomes significant that we protect our anointing for the Anointed One, Christ.

How do we keep and protect with all diligence? We must be careful of our relationship with anything or anyone. My experience in observing and reflecting is that the relationships that we develop and nurture really influence our lives. Whether good or bad, we must be aware of their influence on us. If we relate constructively, the relationship adds to our lives and helps or enhances our relationship with the Holy Trinity; we are better because of it. Yet, we have to be careful to keep our fellowship with God first in our lives. Over time, we can become unconsciously unbalanced in the devotion of more time to another person than we devote to the Lord. This is a very subtle issue. It can happen to us before we know it. Therefore, we must strike a balanced life by putting God first, family second, and work third.

It is amazing that God Himself will allow the best of relationships to go awry when we no longer position Him first in our lives. Moreover, because He loves us and chastens us in love, we are not to despise His correction. He uses relationships to bring His prodigals back to Himself by letting us wallow in the pigsty. When we realize where we are, how we got there, and what created this lowly position of looking like anything but the royalty we are in the Lord, we return to the Father's house. There we find the warmth of God's heart, the soothing and healing of our wounds, the provision we need, and the protection of our anointing. So, we must be careful to balance our relationships and keep our spirit intimate with Him thereby keeping and protecting our anointing.

Secondly, *The Living Bible* states in Proverbs 4:23: "Above all else, guard your affections. For they influence everything else in your life." Our first affection is to be none other than our love for God. Did not the Alpha and Omega say we are to never leave our first love?

> Unto the angel of the church of Ephesus write: These *things* saith He that *holdeth* the seven stars in his right hand, who *walketh* in the midst of the seven golden candlesticks; "*I know* thy works, and thy labor, and thy patience, and how thou canst not bear them that are evil; and thou hast tried them which say they are apostles, and are not, and hast found them

liars: And hast borne, and hast patience, and for my name's sake hast labored, and hast not fainted. Nevertheless I have somewhat against thee, because thou hast left thy first love."
—Revelation 2:1–4

We are never to leave our first love, which is none other than Jesus Christ—not for fame, fortune, power, possessions, positions, or prestige.

We tend to invert our relationship with the Holy God, Jesus our Savior, Comforter, and Keeper, and the Holy Spirit. In the human scheme of life, we seek possessions, position, and power in this earthly realm before we work on an intimate relationship with God which would give us power with Him and influence with man as a result of it. I recall Matthew 6:33: "But seek ye *first* the kingdom of God, and his righteousness; and *all these things* shall be added unto you." Therefore, we need to return to the Rock of Ages that lets us hide ourselves in Him.

My fellow laborers in the Lord, when we leave our first love, it is like not guarding our anointing, like leaving Jesus Christ in us and divorcing the person of the Holy Spirit. If we leave Him, our power to operate in Him weakens; our strength to live righteous and separated or devoted lives weakens. Our will to overcome sin is no longer His because He, who would keep us protected under His wings, experiences our absence from His Presence. Therefore, it is like a husband who protected His family with the emotional, material, and spiritual sustenance forsaking them and leaving them unguarded and unprotected. It is like a wife leaving the shelter of her husband for something strange or unfamiliar. She leaves herself unprotected and vulnerable to the attacks of the Enemy by whoever Satan motivates to strike her in the weakest areas of her personality. A similar experience happens to the husband or father who leaves his family.

Moreover, it is extremely important that we observe how Jesus kept His heart in dealing with the issues of life as well as His greatest affections. Matthew 14:22–23 says: "And straightway Jesus constrained his disciples to get into a ship, and to go before him to the other side, while he sent the multitudes away. And when he had sent the multitudes away, he went up into a mountain *apart* to *pray*: and when the evening had come, he was there alone." Because of His quality time alone with God, He continuously prepared Himself with the power of God as well as the armor of God to deal with the most important issues of life.

Without consistently guarding His heart in time alone with God, Jesus would have been too weak and powerless to confront the daily circumstances of His life. The secret of His power with God and ability to operate as the Flaming Fire of God originated in the time He spent alone with God. Therefore, the Pharisees and Sadducees' accusations of false doctrine were ineffective in throwing Him off the focus of His vision, to redeem fallen humanity. His crucifixion was to give everyone the anointed power of His resurrection from the dead of which Paul spoke: "That I may know him, and the power of his resurrection, and the fellowship of his sufferings, being made conformable unto his death" (Phil. 3:10).

The adversities of this life, the subtle darts that Satan hurls at us, the disappointments and disappointing people in this life, are there to distract us from the goals and visions God has given us to achieve. That is why we must set our affections on the things above and not on the things of the earth. Jesus was aware of the enemy's plot to deceive Him, to redirect His focus. He knew that He had to guard His affections in order to accomplish His mission. He knew that, as stated in Luke 4:18–19: "The Spirit of the Lord is upon me, because he hath anointed me *to preach* the gospel to the poor; he hath sent me to heal the brokenhearted, to preach deliverance to the captives, and recovering of sight *to the blind, to set at liberty* them that are bruised, *to preach* the acceptable year of the Lord." He knew that His affections influenced every area of His life.

These affections were too important for the opinions and doctrines of men to influence them. The gospel had to be preached and taught with such anointed power of God that mankind would not only be hungry and thirsty for it but also would turn to God in repentance and find fulfillment in God's Word. The hungry had to realize that the greatest hunger was not for physical food but the hunger for God. The miracles that God would perform through Jesus, God's available and accessible vessel, would be signs and wonders confirming the Word of God as God's will expressed from God's mind. The twelve disciples had to experience the greatest seminary and Bible school combined into one at His feet.

This was an awesome task. He could not afford to lose sight of His vision because He knew that true theology is only a resource from the Source of the Word of God. Jesus had to mentor the disciples so that they could start the New Testament church, be the vessels of God, and suffer whatever persecution necessary to complete their mission. Jesus had too much to lose to be distracted from His vision. He had to have the energy and inspiration from God each day to work toward the success of His vision. In Genesis 3:15, God mentions Jesus' vision: "And I will put enmity between thee and the woman, and between thy seed and her seed; it shall bruise thy head, and thou shalt bruise his heel." The woman's seed spoken of by God in this prophecy would be none other than Jesus, and He would be born with this vision of crushing Satan's head and putting Him to open shame. In His heart, Jesus' vision was established in Isaiah 53:1–12 before He was born:

> Who hath believed our report? And to whom is the arm of the LORD revealed? For he shall grow up before him as a tender plant, and as a root out of dry ground: he hath no form nor comeliness; and when we shall see him, there is no beauty that we should desire him. He is despised and rejected of men; a man of sorrows, and acquainted with grief: and we hid as it were our faces from him; he was despised, and we esteemed him not. Surely he hath borne our griefs, and carried our sorrows: yet we did esteem him stricken, smitten of God, and afflicted. But he was wounded for our transgressions, he was bruised for our iniquities: the chastisement of our peace was upon him; and with his stripes we are healed. All we like

sheep have gone astray; we have turned every one to his own way; and the LORD hath laid on him the iniquity of us all. He was oppressed, and he was afflicted, yet he opened not his mouth: he is brought as a lamb to the slaughter, and as a sheep before her shearers is dumb, so he openeth not his mouth. He was taken from prison and from judgment: and who shall declare his generation? For he was cut off out of the land of the living: for the transgression of my people was he stricken. And he made his grave with the wicked, and with the rich in his death; because he had done no violence, neither was any deceit in his mouth. Yet it pleased the LORD to bruise him, he hath put him to grief: when thou shalt make his soul an offering for sin, he shall see his seed, he shall prolong his days, and the pleasure of the LORD shall prosper in his hand. He shall see of the travail of his soul, and shall be satisfied: by his knowledge shall my righteous servant justify many; for he shall bear their iniquities. Therefore will I divide him a portion with the great, and he shall divide the spoil with the strong; because he hath poured out his soul unto death: and he was numbered with the transgressors; and he bore the sin of many, and made intercession for the transgressors.

Jesus was not distracted from His God-given vision. Nor must you and I be distracted from our vision or position of authority in Christ. You and I cannot afford to be misled, misdirected, or misplaced by deception from our visions. They may have come to fruition, but our God-given visions have to be protected with all our hearts even as Jesus protected His. This can be done by our power with God, given by God as we consistently spend time in His Presence no matter what it takes. The power of the anointing given to us for our vision also brings responsibility for doing everything we can to achieve God's will and purpose in us.

CHAPTER 6

AN AWESOME
RESPONSIBILITY

Since the success and fulfillment of the Christian ministry originate with God, it stands to reason that God is the source of power and provision for the enormous task to which He directs us. The ministry really is not ours; we are the stewards who are entrusted by God to carry out His mandates under the leadership of the Holy Spirit.

As we trust God for material and earthly possessions, our faith is deeply embedded into our spirits, and we will trust in man and his resources less. God, therefore, becomes the Person we trust. When we understand that the earth is the Lord's and the fullness thereof, the world and they that dwell therein, we will seek first the kingdom of God and His righteousness for all necessary and abundant earthly goods. We should trust man less and trust God more. We should be less sensitive to man's demands and more sensitive to the demands of God's Spirit. "For the eyes of the LORD run to and fro throughout the whole earth, to shew himself strong in the behalf of them whose heart is perfect toward him" (2 Chron. 16:9a).

God seeks ministers who will have the courage, fortitude, and strength to step out from among the crowd of those who do ministry as usual. He looks for men and women who have such reverential trust in His love and care that they will take whatever steps are necessary to follow God. God's eyes are searching the earth for men and women who are sick and tired of being sick and tired of the traditions and doctrines of men making the things of God null and void. When God finds such men and women ministers, even if they are already pastors, He sees ministers that He can use and trust to fellowship with Him in an intimate relationship. He sees servants of God whose hearts are after His own. He sees servants who, if necessary, will leave the traditions of men so that God can set them on fire with the fullness of and baptism in the Holy Spirit.

God's ministers have the awesome responsibility to seek the face of God and His righteousness so diligently that, when God calls one out from the usual modus operandi of Christian service to a deeper and fuller life of the operating in the fullness of His Spirit and the gifts of the Holy Spirit, he will not hesitate to follow Him. There will be only an abiding faith and conviction in his spirit that this is God talking and bidding him to enter into unknown territory.

This kind of faith emboldens one to follow where He leads. We walk by faith and not by sight. We are the just who live by faith. We know that "Without faith it is impossible to please him: for he that cometh to God must believe that he is, and that he is a rewarder of them that diligently seek him" (Heb. 11:6).

Focus a moment on that phrase, "them that diligently seek him." *Diligently* means cravingly, such as one craves food when hungry, so one craves after God when hungry for the Word if he is spiritually famished. Another example would be intense thirst for water or some liquid to quench the thirst. In this same way, we crave the living water of the Word when thirsty for God. In essence, we seek Jesus Christ, our Lord and Savior, when we are nearly out of spiritual strength and inner substance because we have poured the inner strength and spiritual fiber into the lives of others. (This will be elaborated on in a later chapter.)

"As the hart panteth after the water brooks, so panteth my soul after thee, O God. My soul thirsteth for God, for the living God: when shall I come and appear before God?" (Ps. 42:1–2). A male deer, over five years of age, is used here as a metaphor for the spiritual man seeking God. The spirit loves to feed on the living water of the Word of God. When the hunter is chasing the hart, he will stay near the river and stay submerged as long as his breath permits. Similarly, the child of God who knows Jesus as his refuge and fortress stays under the Master Protector's shelter until God permits him to face his enemies again. The hart is often alone; however, the Christian steward of the gospel is never alone when he is in an intimate relationship with God.

The hart swims downstream in the river so as not to touch the branches of the trees and leave a scent for his enemies to follow. Jesus' ministers, whom He develops into flames of fire, must also know how to close the doors of opposition, tactfully and wisely, as they move and have their being in Him. Please understand that Satan's hounds are after the servants of God. First, Satan's hounds want to steal the Word of God, the spiritual nurturance that fulfills the needs and inspires other servants of God to diligently seek Him. Secondly, the hounds are after the anointing on the minister to make it ineffective, for the Spirit's unction gives fellow Christians the authority to operate in the gifts of the Spirit to defeat Satan. Thirdly, the hounds are after the ministries, for these are the organizations that God establishes on earth to save, to edify, and to equip His children.

The hart, by not touching the tree branches, prevents the hounds from picking up his scent. As the hart hides its scent from the dogs, so you and I must use preventative measures to deter the Enemy from attacking. The best preventative measure is the removal of vulnerable opportunities. We must close all doors that are open to the Enemy's (Satan's) weapons. If we are vulnerable to the temptation of adultery and fornication, we must find the comfort, encouragement, and strength in God's verses of Scripture that will fortify us to overcome it. One such

Scripture is 1 Corinthians 10:13: "There hath no temptation taken you but such as is common to man: but God is faithful, who will not suffer you to be tempted above that ye are able; but will with the temptation also make a way of escape, that ye may be able to bear it." God is faithful to His word to show you how to resist your fleshly desires. He will strengthen you to bear it, to overcome it. Take God's way.

Are you strong in this area? Then be reminded, "Wherefore let him that thinketh he standeth take heed lest he fall" (1 Cor. 10:12). Why? My Christian brothers and sisters, all of us are capable of being weak and may yield to temptation—including sex, greed, unfair or unscrupulous business deals, and more. We must take heed lest we fall. We must stay on our toes with God's help. His grace and mercy are sufficient to help us in time of need to overcome the evils of life.

We have to be aware of the test of endurance. Sometimes we are bombarded by the same temptation(s) over a long time. Herein, we have to be careful of the Enemy's scheme to weaken us so that we will surrender to his plots. Satan knows our determination to be unyielding and tenacious in the Lord. The Lord is strong. Therefore, the plot is to touch up us here, to touch up us there, like a man who feels that the woman will give in eventually. Remember also that some women use the same plan! The ultimate strategy is to wear us down so that we shall give up and give in. But in God, there's a remedy straight from His Word. James 1:12 contains the solution: "Blessed is the man that endureth temptation: for when he is tried, *he shall receive* the crown of life, which the Lord hath promised to them that love him."

Fourthly, we must be aware of our thoughts and imaginations. Thoughts and imaginations contain the seeds of temptation. Satan first sends a thought that can develop into imaginations of the reality of the evil with plans fully developed. This is very subtle. Satan is a cunning snake who knows, "When to hold it and when to fold it." God's remedy to sustain us against Satan's assaults is found in 2 Corinthians 10:4–5: "For the weapons of our warfare

are not carnal, but mighty through God to the pulling down of strong holds; *casting down* imaginations, and every high thing that exalteth itself against the knowledge of God, and *bringing into captivity* every thought to the obedience of Christ."

How can we handle imaginations and high things of Satan against our knowledge of God? Simply say, "God, Jesus, or the Holy Spirit, I bring this thought, this imagination against the knowledge of you into the obedience of Jesus Christ." Does it work effectively? Yes, I'm a living witness to that fact. I have used it for years. Sometimes this method has been the only thing that does work. Believe me, the thought goes away; the imagination of plans to do evil flees. When I give in mentally and from my heart to the captivity of obedience of Jesus, the evil thoughts and imaginations quickly leave.

This is a weapon of mighty warfare that is not fleshly to pull down any stronghold on us that Satan uses, has used, or is using against us. God gives us the tools and skills of spiritual warfare to overcome the Enemy so that we can be victorious. As a result of our victory, we can then share the fire of the anointing and the spiritual strategies with others so they, too, can experience victory in their lives in the same ways that we have become winners.

Jesus used the Word of God as the most effective weapon to protect Himself, His anointing, and His fellowship with God. I refer to Matthew 4:1–11. But first, let me state that John the Baptist had just baptized Jesus. More importantly, he had experienced and seen the Holy Spirit descending like a dove and lighting upon Him, and lo, a voice from heaven saying, "This is my beloved Son, in whom I am well pleased" (Matt. 3:17). Be aware, my fellow laborers in God's vineyard, that sometimes after God gives us an anointing or even a fresh anointing, Satan immediately comes to attack or tempt us in the greatest fashion. This is what Satan did as Jesus was led by God after this great anointing:

> Then was Jesus led up of the Spirit into the wilderness to be tempted of the devil. And when he had fasted forty days

and forty nights, he was afterward an hungered. And when the tempter came to him, he said, "If thou be the Son of God, command that these stones be made bread." But he answered and said, "It is written, 'Man shall not live by bread alone, but by every word that proceedeth out of the mouth of God.'" Then the devil taketh him up into the holy city, and setteth him on the pinnacle of the temple, and saith unto him, "If thou be the Son of God, cast thyself down: for it is written, 'He shall give his angels charge concerning thee: and in their hands they shall bear thee up, lest at any time thou dash thy foot against a stone.'" Jesus said unto him, "It is written again, 'Thou shalt not tempt the Lord thy God.'" Again, the devil taketh him up into an exceeding high mountain, and sheweth him all the kingdoms of the world, and the glory of them; And saith unto him, "All these things will I give thee, if thou wilt fall down and worship me." Then saith Jesus unto him, "Get thee hence, Satan: for it is written, 'Thou shalt worship the Lord thy God, and him only shalt thou serve.'" Then the devil leaveth him, and, behold, angels came and ministered unto him.

Based on our past experiences when we were unsaved, Satan is extremely brilliant. Therefore, with the knowledge that Jesus was hungry and possibly very much in need of food after a forty-day fast, the temptation to turn stones into bread was an appeal to satisfy the needs of the flesh. For many men who possessed the power of miracles, this would have been a great temptation. Jesus Christ's wisdom, however, exceeded Satan's brilliance and made Him keenly aware of Satan's wiles.

Satan tried to make Jesus doubt His heritage. The phrase, "*If thou be the Son of God . . .*" was an attack on Christ Jesus' ego. It was Satan's attempt to make Jesus doubt who He was. In fact, Satan repeated the same statement with the second temptation, but Jesus knew who He was in God and in Himself. I submit to you, my colleagues in the ministry, that if Satan can ever get us to doubt who we are in the Lord, especially over a long period of time, He will bring us to some of the lowest levels of decadence of sin that mankind has ever experienced. Far too often, this cunning tactic has been highly successful in the lives of many God-called and sent ministries. Moreover, we must become fully knowledgeable of who we are, whose we are, and our awesome responsibility to Him, and we must hang onto and act upon those truths. These principles need to be adhered to and applied to our lives. Our endeavor should be, not only to be keenly aware today that we are, first, sons and daughters of God, but also we must study to show ourselves approved unto God to attain an ever increasing knowledge of God so that we may know ourselves in His light for ever more. Our endeavor and steady goal should be to know what we have in Him and what we can do with what we have in Him. So be aware, my friends, that this was an emotional and psychological question from the evil prince of the air.

Let us rewind the tape to the temptation: "And when the tempter came to him, he said, 'If thou be the Son of God, command that these stones be made bread'" (Matt. 4:3). Satan knew who Jesus was. He had stayed alert since God's prophecy in Genesis that the seed of woman would bruise Satan's head, but Satan would bruise His heel. This wasn't a threat but a devastating prophecy from the Warrior of all warriors, the most powerful General of all generals. Had God said that to me, I would have believed Him, and you probably would have, also.

When Jesus came to earth, the tempter knew of His conception, and he tried to kill Him through King Herod. The Enemy knows you, too. That is why Satan fights us so hard. He knows we are a powerful threat to his kingdom. He knows that we, by the power and fire of the Holy Ghost, will send demons back to hell. He knows that the goals and visions God has in us will help in destroying his kingdom with violent force. If he wants to continue to reign, Satan has no choice but to fight. *Christians* have no choice but to fight if we want to survive and live abundantly in the Lord under the overshadowing protection of God's wings. He hides our spirit as we dwell and live in Him.

Satan knows the fiery anointing in us is none other than that same Jesus who bruised his head on Calvary's Cross. Even when Jesus went into Satan's domain of hell, he could not keep Him. Satan knows that he could not capture Jesus. He is aware that Jesus, on Calvary, put him to public shame and humiliation. That is why we are strongly tempted in our flesh. Temptation, while getting us to yield to sin, is only the mechanism that starts us on a corrupt journey to worshipping the evil one, the great deceiver. Satan, my friends, is after our anointing. He looks far beyond the temptation to the ultimate goal of making us utterly ineffective in the charge and work God has given us.

Moreover, may I remind you that our tasks are about the Holy Spirit's work of using us as available and accessible vessels to save souls and to edify mentors and nurture them to join the mighty forces of heaven to take over Satan's kingdom. We are involved in a spiritual, moral, psychological, emotional, material, and physical revolution for the Lord. Satan never wants us to become the mighty, military armed forces for Jesus Christ. He wants to keep us ignorant, rotten, and perishing while we are in our earthly tabernacle. He knows that he is not capable of defeating God, so he attempts to use us as scapegoats. Neither you nor I want to be his scapegoats, but that is what the great attacks on brother Job were about. My brothers and sisters, whatever Satan uses to weaken you, to get you to yield to his plans, *resist it*, rebuke it, pull down the strongholds, and bring it to captivity of obedience in Christ Jesus, the greatest Anointed Son of God. Satan will have to flee.

Our awesome position is the head, not the tail. We are part, parcel, and seal of none other than Jesus' body. Therefore, Satan is under our feet, for we are inclusive in Christ's body with His seating at the right hand of God making intercession for us. We sit with Him in Heavenly places. Satan's emissaries, the demons, dwell in the earthly heavenlies; we dwell in the Heaven of heavens. They dwell in hell. Because Satan is under God's feet, he is also under our feet with his demonic host for we dwell in

Christ. We are part of the body of Jesus Christ. Because of this, we have the awesome responsibility of trampling on and over serpents and scorpions that represent demons. Greater are the legions of angels that are with us than the demons that are with Satan, the great tempter, the father of lies and the great deceiver.

During Satan's first attempt to deceive Christ Jesus, he appealed to His physical hunger. "If thou be the Son of God, command that these stones be made bread." Jesus had the skill and power to achieve this miracle, but not only would it have been wasted energy to impress Satan, it was also not part of God's plan. This temptation was about prestige, a powerful temptation that often causes the man or woman of God to be less effective in God's plan for his ministry or position.

The three words that often trip up workers in the vineyard are *prestige, power,* and *possessions*: "the three powerful P's." Satan's first temptation of Christ concerned prestige. *Webster* defines *prestige* as "prominence or influential status achieved through success, renown, or wealth or the power to command admiration in a group, coveted status." Satan's temptation was an effort to get Jesus to use His awesome power to command admiration by impressing him. This was deception. How often are we tempted to strive for great influential status to command the admiration of others by impressing them as to our achievements?

Please do not misunderstand me: There is an innate need in us to be accepted, approved, and recognized by others, but if we are deceived by the Enemy to seek prestige to impress and influence others, our motive is wrong. The objective should be to seek power with Christ, of Christ, and to use His anointing to accomplish our God-given purposes in life. If we do this, God gives us favor with Him and man. The Lord gives our gifts, talents, and abilities room to blossom by providing opportunities as we move and have our being in Him. Power with God gives us power and prestige with man, for it is from Him. You and I have to be careful that we aren't led down "the primrose path" to self-destruction by the need to impress mankind rather than to be impressed by God. This, too, is an awesome responsibility. Yet in our stand with Jesus, we need to proclaim like Him: ". . . Man shall not live by bread alone, but by every word that proceedeth out of the mouth of God" (Matt. 4:4). The Word of God, when used with the believer's authority, is the most effective weapon against the Devil.

The second temptation from Satan to Jesus was about the second P, power. The Devil takes Jesus into the Holy City and positions Him on the highest pinnacle of the temple (church). This position represents power. The Enemy has no new tricks: He tries to use the same cunning methods on Jesus that he used on Eve and Adam. Satan says to Eve in Genesis 3:4–5: "Ye shall not surely die: For God doth know that in the day ye eat thereof, then your eyes shall be opened, and ye shall be as gods, knowing good and evil." *"Ye shall be as gods"* was Satan's appeal to man's desire for power.

We must recognize, with understanding or discernment of spirit, that whenever Satan purports to speak, the purpose is deception. He camouflages the strategy that he used on the first Adam. Jesus, the second Adam, represents an opportunity for redemption by His blood which reconciles man to God. God gave power to the first Adam to have dominion over the living things of the earth. Therefore, possession of power is an innate desire in humans; God gives us power to use positively, not negatively. God expects the saints to use power effectively and constructively, not destructively. God expects His children to use power for the good of all, not a few. God expects Christians to use power in the production of good works, not in abusive ways. We, however, have misunderstood and not appreciated this precious gift; we have abused and misused this awesome gift from God. It is understandable, therefore, why some people aspire for power in ways most destructive to themselves and others.

Too often, the aspiration for power among us who already have the awesome responsibility as God-called and God-sent causes competition and comparison among the brethren, jealousy and division in the body of Christ, and alienation in the community at large. The world observes envy and strife among us. We should be careful to avoid even the appearance of division among us. The church of the Living God cannot be an available and accessible instrument for God to use under His anointed power in these wicked days if we are not united and of one accord.

View these verses in James 3:14–16: "But if ye have bitter envying and strife in your hearts, *glory not*, and lie not against the truth. This wisdom descendeth *not from above*, but is earthly, sensual, devilish. For *where* envying and strife is, there is confusion and every evil work." Since age nineteen when I entered the ministry, I have seen striving for power and influence in ministry that has caused tremendous, disastrous consequences among ministers, churches, and organizations within the church. How can we expect our churches to be together in the Great Commission for our Lord and Savior Christ if we, the leaders, aren't together in Christian unity and agreement? James 5:16 states: "Confess your faults one to another, and pray one for another, that ye may be healed. The effectual fervent prayer of a righteous man availeth much." What is healed as a result of our confessing our faults? We will be healed of the pain, the injuries, the jealousy, envying, strife, and other negative baggage that we, the Christian church and leaders, have lugged around with us for too many years. We need to come together in fervent, effectual prayer as the righteous men and women of God; we need to confess our faults so that our prayers may be answered by God. This will help us become the most powerful spiritual church on earth. This will help us bring the light of Christ to the wicked, dying world. This will help us bring healing to our wounded brothers and sisters in the Lord. We can effect reconciliation among the brethren.

In our awesome responsibility to the Lord, we need kindness. Ephesians 4:31–32 says, "Let all bitterness, and wrath, and anger, and clamour, and evil speaking, be put away from you, with all malice: And *be* ye kind one to another, tenderhearted, forgiving one another, even as God for Christ's sake hath forgiven you." The work of the Lord is kindness and forgiveness among us.

God wants us unified in kindness to each other, tender-hearted and forgiving one another, even as God has forgiven us for Christ's sake. He wants us unified in kindness, "For the perfecting of the saints, for the work of the ministry, for the edifying of the body of Christ: till we all come in the unity of faith, and of the knowledge of the Son of God, unto a perfect man, unto the measure of the stature of the fullness of Christ" (Eph. 4:12–13). This may appear idealistic because of our different denominations, creeds, and religions. Yet if the Bible says that unity in the Lord is the purpose for different ministries, then it must be, because, in the final analysis, God must be true and every man a liar if necessary.

When God called and gave us our awesome responsibility, He empowered us to stand in the gap for and to minister to kings, queens, presidents, millionaires, billionaires, and potentates as a serviceable position to the highest and the lowest, the richest and the poorest. God gave us prestige and power at the very instant He called us.

In the ministry to which we are stewards, God has made us watchmen over all of mankind. Father God said to Ezekiel, "Son of man, I have made thee a watchman unto the house of Israel: therefore hear the word at my mouth, and give them warning from me" (Ezek. 3:17). As Ezekiel's ministry was to Israel, so is our ministry to the nations of the earth. We are in a lofty place as God's flames of fire, not as lords over God's heritage but as examples to the flock. From this lofty place as watchmen from the wall and tower, we need not fear man, his words, nor his looks, for we represent Him who has all power and the greatest countenance. "And thou, son of man, be not afraid of them, neither be afraid of their words, though briers and thorns be with thee, and thou dost dwell among scorpions: be not afraid of their words, nor be dismayed at their looks, though they be a rebellious house" (Ezek. 2:6).

Is it not amazing that God has already given us what we strive for—prestige, power, and position? Many of our physical ailments, mental conditions, and psychosomatic illnesses would not exist if we believed and claimed the promises of God for ourselves. He is ready to give us what many of us seek in ministry; the Word of God says in Psalm 75:6–7, "For promotion cometh neither *from* the east, nor from the west, *nor from* the south. But God is the judge: He putteth down one *and setteth* up another." And Proverbs 22:29 says, "*Seest thou* a man diligent in his business? *He shall stand* before kings; he shall not stand before mean men." Diligence in the Lord's work creates promotional opportunities for us, no matter what we call our ministries. So let us be Christlike in endeavoring for the position God has already given us. Let us not strive to attain the three P's. Striving is a misdirected strategy used by the worldly person who does not know the Lord.

Last, but certainly not least, the third temptation offered by the prince of the air was all three P's in one. Remember the camouflaged old tricks? The Enemy apparently felt that if he couldn't deceive Him with the first and second temptations, he would combine them all into one:

> Again, the devil taketh him up into an exceedingly high mountain, and sheweth him all the kingdoms of the world, and the glory of them; and saith unto Him, "All these things will I give thee, if thou wilt fall down and worship me." Then saith Jesus unto him, "Get thee hence, Satan; for it is written, 'Thou shalt worship the Lord thy God, and him only shalt thou serve.'" Then the devil leaveth him, and, and behold, angels came and ministered unto him.
> —Matthew 4:8–11

Satan's major focus here is on possession, and this area has caused more havoc in the church of God and among our leaders than prestige and position combined. We must possess prestige in order to wield it. We must possess position in order to use it. Possession is the most dangerous of the three P's.

The adversary's temptation was designed to be destructive. His work is always destructive, and his purposes are always disastrous. Jesus speaks to us in Luke 12:15: "And he said unto them, 'Take heed, and beware of covetousness: for a man's life consisteth not in the abundance of things which he possesseth.'" Satan does not care if we are deceived in setting goals for material or abstract things; as long as our objective isn't God-centered and God-led, we are on his turf. What a terrible playing field! You and I can never win on Satan's turf without God. This was Satan's attempt with Jesus, but our Lord knew with whom he was dealing. He had put on the whole amour of God and was not going to fall into this snare. Neither does He want us to fall into Satan's trap as we carry out our awesome responsibility. Yet, we have fallen frequently for this wile of the Devil.

I have discovered that when my goals are not Christ-centered, they are hardest to achieve. If I do reach them, the hard work, the pain, the stress, and the strain of obtaining them have worn me out, and I become vulnerable to the Enemy's attack. It has been a very hard lesson, but I have learned it in time to close the windows of opportunity to the demons. Yet, I have to admit that the natural man wants possessions to satisfy his physical and soulful needs. The caution to us is to always focus on Jesus' admonition to us: "But seek ye first the kingdom of God, and his righteousness; and all these things shall be added unto you. Take therefore no thought for the morrow: for the morrow shall take thought for the things of itself. Sufficient unto the day is the evil thereof" (Matt. 6:33–34).

Moreover, we have to be very careful to strike this balance of possessions for the natural life and possession of the spiritual things for the nourishment and nurturance of our spirit. If we get the wisdom of God with understanding because of diligent quality time with God—fasting, prayer, and intimate fellowship with Jesus—Father God will bless us with the possessions. And we will certainly enhance our balance in life. The key here is that we possess things. Things should never possess us.

Besides, Paul said it so very well in Philippians 4:19: "But my God shall supply all your need according to his riches in glory by Christ Jesus." As to the things we want along with our necessities, David said it also in Psalm 37:4–5: "Delight thyself also in the LORD; and he shall give thee the desires of thine heart. Commit thy way unto the LORD; trust also in him; and he shall bring it to pass." These are the keys to the needs and desires of God-centered and God-directed possessions, delighting in the Lord, and committing our way to Him.

Most importantly, Jesus did just that in quiet, quality time with God. Matthew 14:22–23 says, "And straightway Jesus constrained his disciples to get into a ship, and to go before him unto the other side, while he sent the multitudes away. And when he had sent the multitudes away, he went up into a mountain apart to pray; and when the evening was come, he was there alone." Our Savior left us the model for having power with God, power in God for the day and for our acquisition of things. He went apart, to separate Himself for time with God. Therefore, He was prepared and committed to God each day for whatever came His way even from the devices of man and Satan. He walked in the anointing, lived in the anointing by being sensitive to the Spirit of God's direction and leadership.

Each day for Jesus was a day of victory, including the day He hung on the Cross. He put our greatest foe to shame and humiliation by making him a public spectacle on that day. The crucifixion of Jesus defeated Satan. Jesus Christ's resurrection from the dead sealed Satan's defeat. Our victory over destructive prestige, position, and possessions lies in the example of Jesus. Spend quiet, quality time with God and use the powerful authority of His Word. Our key to walking in the anointing, as exemplified by our Lord, lies in spending time with God and in His presence. Our most important objective should be power with God, and He will give us constructive power and favor with man.

One of the secrets of Jesus' power with God and man was His pure lifestyle. He learned obedience by the things He suffered. We, too, must understand that part of the foundation for our power with God and man is our pure lifestyle that supports our ministries. Therefore, we must yield to the purging process at God's hands.

CHAPTER 7

THE PURGING PROCESS

The Holy Spirit may shake and break us to eliminate or purge everything from our lives that would hinder the powerful flow of Him into our ministry. I am reminded of Jesus' discourse on the true Vine and the branches in John 15:1–7:

> I am the true vine, and my Father is the husbandman. Every branch in me that beareth not fruit he taketh away: and every branch that beareth fruit, he purgeth it, that it may bring forth more fruit. Now ye are clean through the word which I have spoken unto you. Abide in me, and I in you. As the branch cannot bear fruit of itself, except it abide in the vine; no more can ye, except ye abide in me. I am the vine, ye are the branches: He that abideth in me, and I in him, the same bringeth forth much fruit: for without me ye can do nothing. If a man abide not in me, he is cast forth as a branch, and is withered; and men gather them, and cast them into the fire, and they are burned. If ye abide in me, and my words abide in you, ye shall ask what ye will, and it shall be done unto you.

As the Holy Spirit leads me, may I attempt to analyze this passage? Jesus is depicting Himself as the true Vine in which we dwell as the branches. Father God is the Husbandman, the

Vinedresser. As the Tiller of the soil, God plows the ground, sows seeds in the ground, and nourishes with the water of the Word of God, so the Vine can grow to fullness of life to produce. The Vine and its branches get the life-giving strength from the growing power of the Word that Jesus has spoken to the church, the branches. The branches are an extension of the Vine, Jesus; in the purging process, God prunes, cuts, or breaks off every branch that does not produce fruit. The pruned branch will be even more productive. Notice verse three, we become clean through the Word that Jesus has spoken, speaks, and will speak to us. The principle is heart cleansing.

During a very crucial period in my life, nothing seemed to be working out for me. Neither resources, friends, nor material goods were effective; God was at work in my circumstances to effect an inner cleansing, a heart purging to bring me to absolute dependence on Him. Without my knowledge or consent, God was doing what He had desired to do for years, but I had to come to the end of my rope. There I found myself in danger of failure in every area of my life.

At this point, only one thing was important—my faith that Jesus would intercede from the right hand of God for my faith in the Holy Spirit who would see that my prayers were received by Jesus and in God, my Father, who would receive prayers being offered to Him from the heart and hand of Jesus. I did not know it, but God was in the process of bringing about a tremendous change in the emphases and direction in my life.

This change included days alone with Christ, my Lord, and I still want to spend days alone with Christ. During this time, however, I was constantly in God's Word, the written Word of God that was cleansing and purging me from the inside. I do remember that I wasn't doing anything that was obviously sinful. Sin, I learned during this experience, may not be causing external harm to one's self or others; it can be a terrible and excruciating thing of the heart. I was alone with Jesus, the Holy Spirit, and God, constantly in the Word. The Spirit of God led me to pray constantly. As I prayed, God did something that has become a most cherished, valuable, and useful tool in my walk with Him.

Father God showed me the George who I was as He perceived me in my heart. The process of inner purging operated effectively in my heart for days. Father God showed me things—inner weaknesses, inner sins of my heart—that I found unimaginable. Yet, I know this was God at work on me and in me. I could not deny the convincing and the convicting of sins in my heart. The hurt, in confronting me for who I was, was real. There was no avoiding issues with God; there was no self-denying, no blocking out, no sticking my head in the sand as an ostrich that does not want to face the real dangers in life. This was I! In this time with God, as I faced myself, in the eyes of God, I cried continuous tears in confessing my sins and contritely repenting of them. I say to you, my brothers and sisters in the ministry, and to others who would seek to truly minister as one of God's flames of fire, that this experience of confronting the truth hurt, but it was also defining. God revealed another powerful principle of His Word and Himself: Because I was allowing Him to purify me, He would answer my prayers quickly and effectively.

There were times when, after confession and repentance of sin, I would ask God for certain blessings. He would answer my prayers so quickly that sometimes I did not realize He had given me the blessing I prayed for until I had already walked through or experienced it. This amazed me!

What was God doing in this purging process? Surely, I was in the Refiner's fire; God was cleansing me on the inside to effect a change on the outside. According to Jesus, clean the inside of the dish first and then the outside. This process went on for days. As I confessed, confessed, confessed, repented, repented, and repented with crying—even more than when my earthly father died, God was leading me into a continuous faith walk with Him. God was leading me to be filled with His Spirit, to teach and preach the full counsel of His Word as He would lead me to operate in the gifts of the Holy Ghost. Teaching, preaching, healing, and passing the infilling of His Spirit to others became paramount in my pastoral ministry.

I told a colleague: "I must do this or die." His response was, "God doesn't want you to die, George; He just wants you to fulfill His will." I learned, as a result of the Refiner's fire experience, the blessings of purging even for a pastor.

Jesus said, "Abide in me, and I in you. As the branch cannot bear fruit of itself, except it abide in the vine; no more can ye, except ye abide in me" (John 15:4). I learned to abide, to rest in, to sit in, and to dwell in Jesus. I also learned to bear fruit in the Holy Spirit as Jesus and I abode in each other.

The anointing of the Holy Spirit became powerful in teaching, healing, and baptism in the Holy Spirit in the church. I recall one particularly vivid experience of healing. When I returned from vacation, I was told that one of the church's deaconesses had experienced a massive heart attack and was in Duke Hospital. For a couple days while I caught up the church workload, I was unable to visit her. Before I visited her on Monday, another full gospel pastor said to me, "Cromwell, go on in the Spirit, anyway, and lay on hands in Jesus' name." In the sister's hospital room, amid her complaints about the intravenous tubes, I asked her if she minded my praying for her with the laying on of hands. She said, "No." Then I prayed, laid on hands, and left her hospital room. Even though the Spirit did not overcome her, when I was five minutes from the hospital, the Spirit of God anointed my head with intensity, confirming this sister's healing.

The next morning, I called the sister's hospital room. No one answered the phone, so I called the front desk nurses' station. They said that she was not a patient there. I called her home, and she informed me that the doctors examined her Monday night, removed the intravenous tubes, and released her from the hospital the next morning. They "didn't know what happened."

What was God's process?

- First, He allowed me to come to a point in life of absolute and total dependence, by faith, in Him.
- Second, He, within the trials by fire experiences (circumstances) in my life, showed me myself with sins of my heart.
- Third, He convinced and convicted me of sin.
- Fourth, He demanded that I confess and repent of inner-man sins.
- Fifth, I confessed and sincerely repented.
- Sixth, God purged and purified me.
- Seventh, He answered my prayers immediately, often without my recognizing the answer until after it was received and experienced. Before my purging experience, I would have recognized the blessing before experiencing an answered prayer.
- Eighth, God in-filled me again and baptized me with the Holy Spirit.
- Ninth, He gave me new direction of ministry in teaching and preaching the gospel with the fire of the Holy Spirit accompanied by operating in the gifts of the Holy Spirit.

I thank God for this purging, the purification, and the abiding in Jesus process. Let me add an extremely important note here, my friends in the Lord:

- The tenth step in this whole process was *obedience*, obedience to the Spirit of God.

I have never regretted God's call for this new direction in my life and ministry. This way of faith, of fullness with His Holy Spirit, is most satisfying and fulfilling. This is greater than happiness. I learned to abide in the Vine, Jesus. I learned, as God's child, to be obedient to the Father. Obedience is my choice and decision, and it allows Jesus to abide in me. (Praise God, Praise God, Praise God. Alleluia, Lord of Lords, to Him who sits upon the Throne of Heaven, whose cloud filled the Temple, whose robe is most majestic.)

I have always wanted everything that the Lord Jesus has to offer. Jesus said, in verse 4, "Abide in me, and I in you. As the branch cannot bear fruit of itself, except it abide in the vine; no more can ye, except ye abide in me." This truth had to become real to me in my own experiences as a pastor. Before my purging experience, I said to myself: "There has to be more to pastoring than just teaching, preaching, and administering a church." Few people were saved. Something was missing.

I recalled Zechariah 4:6: "Then he answered and spake unto me, saying, 'This is the word of the Lord unto Zerubbabel, saying, Not by might, nor by power, but by my Spirit, saith the LORD of hosts.'" Because I was abiding in Christ as one of the branches and He was abiding in me as the Vine, I had a revelation. If we were going to save souls in the church, if we were going to have an effective ministry and not just a successful renovation program at the church, I would have to depend on the Word of God coming alive in the ministry as I became an inward and outward doer of it. The Spirit of God, working through me to effectively or powerfully minister to the people, would bring about the increase.

The membership increased, the power of God manifested itself, and the congregation experienced His presence. This was a result of self-realization in the Lord—of His Word abiding in me, of my abiding in Him, and in His Anointing on me. Overall, the purification process was still operating in my life and ministry. The movement of God's Spirit in His church included me.

I had come to realize verse 5: Jesus is the giver of life, a living, growing vine of the church and its ministry, my ministry of which I am only a steward. I had to be faithful in His calling in my personal life, public life, and professional work. I was only abiding in Him, the Vine. Without Him I would be ineffective and weak. In reality, I could do nothing unless I abode in

Him and faithfully depended on the Holy Spirit's work in and through me. I could not afford to be cut, broken, or pruned off the vine and put aside. I could not afford a lifeless ministry and meaningless life; therefore, I had to abide in Jesus and allow the Holy Spirit to take *the lead* in my ministry.

The purpose for my life and work had to be greater than my personal purpose. The plan had to be more important than any plan that I could conceive. Both purpose and plan had to transcend anything I could bring about in or by myself. God saw this and gave me a vision to serve Him beyond any goal I had ever set and achieved. I found a motivation and inspiration to serve far above and beyond anything I could ever imagine. He gave me the desires of my heart that *are really His desires for me*. I learned to abide in Him, and I learned to be blessed by Him and still grow in knowledge and understanding. By abiding in Him, *I can ask what I will, and it shall be done unto me.*

These truths and the knowledge gained from God during some of the most crucial and excruciating experiences in life allow me to do all the things that God wants me to do as He strengthens me. My desire is to become continuously, and most powerfully, set on fire by His Spirit so that He can do things with me and through me far beyond and abundantly above those that I could ask or think.

The process of purification and purging does not cease. It is a continuous process as God takes off ineffective things that might appear to us most important but to Him are least essential in His divine plan and purpose for us. As I understand it, *the divine purpose in this life for all of our lives is to glorify God and to enjoy Him forever*. We must teach and preach this to those who have lost hope and have no meaningful purpose in life. This must spread to the masses of people whom God would have His flames of fire to serve.

Moreover, after God finishes shaking and pruning, or purging us, there is another process we must experience sometime in our lives, if we have previously not come to this position. This process is the shaping and molding that Father God desires to bring about in our lives. We are His children. A good parent instills morals, values, and constructive principles in rearing his offspring that should shape and mold their lives and their lifestyle. The lifestyle, of course, is the way they live and the levels of life to which they rise. I refer us to Jeremiah 18:1–10:

> *The word* which came to Jeremiah from the LORD, saying, "Arise, and go down to the potter's house, and there I will cause thee to hear my words." Then I went down to the potter's house, and, behold, he wrought a work on the wheels. And the vessel he made of clay was marred in the hand of the potter: so he made it again another vessel, as seemed good to the potter to make it. *Then the word of the Lord came to me,* saying, "O house of Israel, cannot I do with you as this potter?" saith the LORD. "Behold, as the clay is in the potter's hand, so are ye in mine hand, O house of Israel. At what instant I shall speak concerning a nation, and concerning a kingdom, to pluck up, and to pull down, and to destroy it; If that nation, against whom I have pronounced, turn from their evil, I will repent of the evil I thought to do unto them. And at what instant I shall speak concerning a nation, and concerning a kingdom, to build and to plant it, If it do evil in my sight, that it obey not my voice, then I will repent of the good, wherewith I said I would benefit them."

As we analyze this passage of Scripture, I pray for the divine revelation of God through Christ the Anointed One. For this passage is so vital to our existence during our fiery trials of faith. As I understand God better, the eyes of my spirit are enlightened to know the hope of His calling. He allows me to know the riches of the glory of His inheritance in His saints—us. Therefore, I am seeking what is the exceeding greatness of His power toward us who believe, according to the working of His mighty power *in proportion to His Word in us as we apply our faith to be doers of His Word.*

First, God commanded that Jeremiah go to the potter's house where God's Word would come to Him. Jeremiah did not hesitate or question God. He had so intimately walked and talked with God that he knew that the Chief Shepherd of the Sheep had spoken directly to his heart. Without question, Jeremiah was instantly sensitive to God's voice and will: "Arise, and go down to the potter's house, and there I will cause thee to hear my words." Jeremiah, in obedience to God and sensitivity to His Spirit, immediately moves according to God's timing and goes to the potter's house. It is important to be sensitive to God's voice, to move immediately when He says to move, to go where He sends us, and to receive the revelation of the Lord in our hearts and lives.

Jeremiah arrives at the potter's house, and he observes a skilled craftsman at work on his wheels preparing a vessel for the Master's use. The vessel that the potter is making is marred. Since it is not a perfect specimen, the potter begins again to make another vessel.

Before dealing with the tremendously powerful symbolism of this scene, let me discuss the potter's wheels and the fate of marred clay in the hands of a proficient craftsman. There are two wheels on this machine. The lower wheel, operated by the feet, moved the upper wheel on a flat disc. On this disc, the potter used his powerful fingers to mold the clay as the wheel rapidly revolved. If a vessel appeared disfigured, warped, or ugly to the potter, he could not display or sell it. Excellence was the standard for his work, and he would not offer anything that did not meet his quality control standards.

The potter had a reputation for the very best quality of any potter in the world. He was not going to risk his good name for one vessel. He did not discard the marred vessel. Instead, he crushed the clay and returned it to the wheel. His work on the vessel began again. This continued until the clay took the shape that the potter desired, and God declared that He would do the same for Israel, His chosen vessel.

In interpreting this passage, I recognize God as the Potter at the wheel. The clay is Israel, but it can also represent us, the church of the Living, Omnipotent, Omnipresent, and Omniscient God. The clay might also represent each one of us personally as individual, distinct personalities or as each God-called and/ or sent minister to become a flaming fire. Unless God shapes, molds, and makes us into His vessels, we never realize our full potential in Him. We will go to our graves or meet Jesus face to face not having saved and influenced the lives that God sent us to serve. Our fruit will not be as bountiful and productive unless we, the clay, yield to the Potter. Therein is the providence of God to do with us as He sees fit.

We have not finished with the scene featuring the potter. God is at the wheel, and the clay is representative of our lives. We are the clay possessed by God, and whether we like it or not, He is in control. He possesses us; He created our bodies. Our souls are worthless without Him. Our hearts are as nothing without His Spirit within them. God bought us with the priceless blood of Jesus. He paid it all for us, and all to Him we owe. Jesus washed the crimson stain of sin as white as snow. Praise and glorify God!

The wheels on the potter's machine represent the two parts of our lives. There are two wheels on this machine and two wheels in our lives. One wheel represents our self-centered lives, and the other represents our spiritual lives. Each wheel contributes to our destiny and has a powerful effect upon our lives. These wheels make the difference between failure and success, defeat or victory, poverty and prosperity or abundant prosperity.

One may ask, "How do you separate the two in that they are seemingly intrinsically intertwined?" My attempt is not on my own but by the Spirit of God. Moreover, I depend on and solicit the help of God in this task. The Bible says, "For the Word of God is quick, and powerful, and *sharper than* any *twoedged* sword, *piercing* even to the *dividing* asunder of soul and spirit, and of the joints and marrow, and is a *discerner* of the thoughts and intents of the heart" (Heb. 4:12).

We are body, soul, and spirit. The Bible says in John 6:63, "It is the spirit that quickeneth; the flesh profiteth nothing: *the words that I speak* unto you, *they are spirit, and they are life.*" The soul and spirit dwell within our bodies; the body is the shell that contains (houses) the soul and spirit. The only real benefits it receives are the satisfaction and fulfillment the soul and spirit receive. Therefore, without the soulish and spiritual benefits, the body—an enclosure we cannot do without in the natural life—has no real purpose except to house our soul and spirit. God, therefore, focuses on the selfish desires and spiritual lives that determine the body's path. It is our *soul*, the seat of our feelings, desires, and appetites, and the *mind*, the thoughts and intents of the innermost being, our spirit or heart, that the Spirit of God discerns and divides. God does this by the Word of God that is *quick*, and powerful and sharper than any two-edged sword. In fact, God's Word is the sharpest sword of our spiritual warfare. It affects the body—joints and marrow—and discerns our most secret thoughts and the intents of our heart and our spirit.

Now our selfish life is the wheel that fights against our spiritual lives. It took time for us to establish our self-centered life and the spiritual life we live in this body. The soul has a tremendous appetite for feelings of pleasure that could fulfill the lust of the flesh, the lust of the eye, and the pride of life. It vehemently opposes the desires of the spirit in each person for satisfaction, fulfillment, and peace with God. Of course, the soul strongly fights the fulfillment of the spirit-man, yielding its will to the will of God according to the Word of God. That is why we may call this a struggle between the twin lives within us. The twins, the soul and spirit, fight each other, and depending on which twin wins, determines the subjection of the body. I ask you, my brothers and sisters, not to disregard this most important inner conflict within you. Each one of us has this fight going on inside us, has had it, or will have it. This struggle is part of the ultimate goal to yield our body, mind, soul, and spirit completely and absolutely to God.

Paul the apostle was quite knowledgeable of this *in-house struggle*. This is where we live; this is where we either yield to sin and therefore to the weakness of the flesh or to the Spirit of God and become doers of His Word. If we yield to God, we are empowered more with His Spirit and anointing. Yielding to God represents victory over the sin that seeks to drive us to self-destruction. This inner struggle determines the destiny of our souls. It will also determine how many souls receive the Spirit of God working through us using His power and might—not ours.

Why does victory over sin determine the soul's destiny? Victory over sin means we have allowed the Holy Spirit to cleanse us of the impurities of our flesh and soul. Victory over sin means greater enlightenment or clarity for our spirit to perceive and receive the revelations of God to impart to the hearts of men. Victory over sin means we have come to a level in our walk in the Spirit that we feed on the Word of God as though our very spiritual growth and lives depend on this spiritual food. We cannot grow without the spiritual food of God's Word. Victory over sin means that we are empowered by God's Anointing in our work to inspire others to achieve God's will on earth. Victory over sin means God has or is or will create in us clean hearts and renew a right spirit within us. God restores the joy of our salvation and upholds us with His free Spirit. Consequently, as we teach transgressors God's ways, sinners are converted to Him.

Sometimes it is impossible to rise to a certain position until we realize how the inner struggle holds us back. Therein is the need for discussion of this conflict. For this discussion, I refer to Romans 7:12–25:

> Wherefore the law is holy, and the commandment holy, and just, and good. Was then that which is good made death unto me? God forbid. But sin, that it might appear sin, working death in me by that which is good; that sin by the commandment might become exceeding sinful. For we know that the law is spiritual: but I am carnal, sold under sin. For that which I do I allow not: but for what I would, that I do not; but

which I hate, that do I. If then I do that which I would not, I consent unto the law that it is good. Now then it is no more I that do it, but sin that dwelleth in me. For I know that in me (that is, in my flesh) dwelleth no good thing: for to will is present within me; but how to perform that which is good I find not. For the good that I would I do not: but the evil which I would not, that I do. Now if I do that I would not, it is no more I that do it, but sin that dwelleth in me. I find then a law, that, when I would do good, evil is present with me. For I delight in the law of God after the inward man: But I see another law in my members, warring against the law of my mind, and bringing me into captivity to the law of sin which is in my members. O wretched man that I am! Who shall deliver me from this body of death? I thank God through Jesus Christ our Lord. So then with the mind I serve the law of God; but with the flesh the law of sin.

This passage deals with the apostle Paul, whose credits include writing at least thirteen books in the New Testament. Why did the powerful, overwhelming anointing of Jesus flow so abundantly through him that he could author such inspiring Scriptures? He penned some of his most powerful words during intense spiritual warfare and persecution. Would-be flames of fire for our Savior can learn some important principles from the life of Paul. Paul had to master himself, his flesh, his soul, and his spirit. Mother used to say to us, her three children, "Your worst enemy is yourself." This is true! I can allow negative circumstances over which I have no control to affect me or I can make the best decision possible with the information that I have. The choice is mine and mine alone. I can defeat negativity in my inner man. As a man thinks, so is he, and I have learned that at least 50 percent of victory over the world, the flesh, and the Devil is won when I am victorious over my thoughts and feelings.

The inner struggle, the tug of war of Romans 7:12–25, is the battle that we must win so that God may shape, mold, and make us into vessels of honor meet for the Master's use in any circumstance. But even as the alcoholic's first step toward healing is often his realization and confession that he's an alcoholic, so must we realize that sometime in this life and often ongoing, we struggle with our soul and spirit. The soul wants to fulfill its appetite for anything that satisfies it, too often trying anything except the things of God. The spirit within us desires to fulfill God's perfect will, in revelation, according to God's Word so that we might be doers of His Word. In the midst of our best endeavors to follow God in the middle of stresses and strains, the soulish desires rise up and say to us, "Take a break, give yourself some sinful leisurely pleasure. You deserve it. Look at all you have done and are doing in service to God. Aren't you tired? Let up! Let go. Loosen up; let your hair down. You deserve it. In fact, you earned it." This was Paul's struggle; he found himself in bondage to sin.

He said it so well: "For that which I do I allow not: for what I would, that do I not, but what I hate, that do I." This is true self-realization, true confession from one of history's greatest spiritual warriors. Paul realized that he had conflicting desires within himself. He says that the sin that he does is not what he wants to do; his spirit disagrees with it. On the other hand, the good that his spirit desires, he does not do. Therefore, his soul controls him, and he does things that his spirit hates. Then Paul said, in today's terms, if I yield to this soulish twin and do that which my spirit does not consent to, according to the mirror of the law of sin, it is good. Yet, I do not like it. I do not agree with it because I do not take my salvation in Jesus as a license to sin. I do not deceive myself in this manner. My spirit really divorces itself from what my soulish-sinful desire permits and does. I confess that it is sin in me.

This is the first step to recovery from sin, sickness, and possible spiritual death. He confesses that sin dwells in him. Therefore, he's well on the way to deliverance in Christ Jesus, whatever the sin or sins he finds himself unable to control. He states in Romans 7:18 that he has had a revelation: no good thing dwells in Paul's flesh. The will to do right is present, but he has not yet learned how to perform right in Christ. For when he would do good, evil is present in him. Now he says: if I do that which I should not do, the law of sin in me rules me. It is too effective for me. Therefore, evil is running its course. What a struggle! What turmoil resides in the inner man. In verse 22, however, he begins to find some delight in the law of God, the Law of Moses mirroring himself after his inward man.

Perhaps I need to pause and say that there are two laws at work here: First, there was the law of sin in his soul. When Paul yielded to his soulish appetites to fulfill them, this law controlled him, and he sinned. Second, there was the law of God that showed Paul himself as a man subjected to sin. The law of God reinforced the fact that Paul would not find any relief in being a morally strict legalist. The law could not liberate him for being a good person; in fact, it would compound his bondage. Moreover, in the midst of this wrestling within himself, he tires of his spirit, his conscience, and God reminding him of his sinful state. He senses self-defeat.

We also must sense our impending self-defeat when we give in to sin. For sin comes to steal, kill, and destroy. Satan uses defeat to prevent us from doing the will of God with the mighty power of God.

Thank God, and praise Him for allowing Paul to be an example for us in demonstrating the way out of our inner-man struggle. Listen to these verses, my Christian brothers and sisters. Paul cries out in anguish of his spirit: "O wretched man that I am! Who shall deliver me from this body of death? I thank God through Jesus Christ our Lord. So then with the mind I myself serve the law of God; but with the flesh the law of sin" (Rom. 7:24–25).

In essence, the soul and spirit are the inner twins that (conflict) fight each other as the wheels. The outcome of this inner conflict determines our growth, promotion, position, and destiny in life. Because the soul is carnally minded, it can bring forth death to our growth in the Lord. It can prevent our greatest development in the Lord and therefore cause the marring in the Potter's hand. Sin displeases God because sin or sins cause disfiguration in the vessel. However, if the clay, the would-be flame of fire for God, will yield his spirit in subjection to God, victory over our soulish, strong desire to sin results in our subjecting ourselves to deliverance by Jesus Christ.

Why does this happen? It happens because of the merciful love of God, the Potter. It happens because God's loving kindness motivates Him to take the marred clay into His hands again. It happens because of God's grace—no matter what stresses, strains, pressures, situations, or negative consequences have caused the marring in our lives. God, with His providential hand, crushes the clay so that He can take the good parts of the old clay and mix it with new clay to make vessels of honor meet for the Master's use in ways that please Him.

God still wants us, brothers and sisters. He still wants the best for us even in the midst of His permissive and perfect will. His primary objective is to bring us to the position of His perfect will. Herein, the vessel has yielded his soul in subjection to His Spirit. Herein, the vessel, with spirit controlling his soul, yields to his Merciful-Loving God all that he has and all that he hopes to be for the shaping, molding, and making that God desires over his desires. Jesus said it so well in Matthew 26:39: "And he went a little farther, and fell on his face, and prayed, saying, 'O my Father, if it be *possible*, let this cup pass from me; nevertheless not as I will, but as thou wilt.'" Therein Jesus submitted His soul in subjection to the will and knowledge of His Spirit that the will of God was more important than anything He desired to do. We must do the same to be most effective in the work God has called us to perform. "For we are his workmanship, created in Christ Jesus unto good works, which God hath before ordained *that* we should walk in them" (Eph. 2:10).

Paul recognized that his real deliverance lay not in himself but in Christ Jesus' power to deliver him from the hindrances of his inner negative nature of the soul. Therefore, as he yielded himself to this major revelation from God, his success lay in what he submitted himself to Christ Jesus in God to do. The determining factor in the Master's proficient hand is absolute surrender to the *Potter's will*.

CHAPTER 8

HIS SURRENDER TO GOD

The anointing is God's requirement for us to become His powerful ministers. The anointing of His Holy Spirit is for doing the work of Christ upon the earth. "Verily, verily, I say unto you, he that believeth on me, the works that I do shall he do also; and greater works than these shall he do; because I go unto my Father" (John 14:12).

The prerequisite for the anointing is drawing nigh to God and staying near Him in purity, sanctification, and holiness. This is where the fire, the burning of God, is located. The Lord is the Glory of God.

> And I saw as the colour of amber, as the appearance of fire round about within it, from the appearance of his loins even upward, and from the appearance of his loins even downward. I saw as it were the appearance of fire, and it had brightness round about. As the appearance of the bow that is in the cloud in the day of rain, so was the appearance of the brightness round about. This was the appearance of the likeness of the glory of the LORD. And when I saw it, I fell upon my face, and I heard a voice of one that spake.
>
> —Ezekiel 1:27–28

We must stay near God and His glory to receive the greatest blessings and revelations for ourselves. These must be instilled in our hearts for them to become an experience that is shared effectively by application in our preaching and teaching to our people. Otherwise, we are imparting head knowledge as though it were heart knowledge.

Another of God's requirements is that we receive the Word of God willingly and openly in our hearts. We must apply the Word of God in our lives so that it will be productive in setting Satan's captives—of every creed, religion, and ethnicity—free. There are many to whom God would send each of us to serve. When we give the Word of God to others, it must become flames of fire to burn up the sin in their hearts so that they can experience the goodness of God, be redeemed by the blood of the Lamb, baptized and in-filled with God's Spirit, and set on the straight path to God and Jesus Christ. It is "Not by might, nor by power, but by my spirit, saith the LORD of hosts" (Zech. 4:6).

God's divine power must strengthen us to do His work and will. Though discouragement comes, we must encourage ourselves with God's Word. Though the gates of hell attempt to stop us, we must put on the full armor of God and go on in His strength and, having done all, stand in His power against all the wiles (strategies) of the Enemy. We must use the Word of God as a flaming two-edged sword against all the host of Satan.

We must intervene against sin. Salvation is God's intervention against man's ruining himself and others. We must yield our bodies to God so that they are living sacrifices, holy and acceptable unto God. We must be ready when God wants to use us as He desires, not when we want to be used. He will use us as flames of fire to do His perfect will as laborers in His vineyard. The hand of the Lord must be upon us to do His work: "So the spirit lifted me up, and took me away, and I went in bitterness, in the heat of my spirit; but the hand of the LORD was strong upon me" (Ezek. 3:14).

We must be God's watchmen. The watchman is one who looks out, or sees from a height, to warn of impending danger or to give good or bad information. Priests or prophets of the Lord were called watchmen. We, too, are watchmen for the souls and spirits of man. We warn them about and provide spiritual tools to protect them from Satan (Ezek. 3:17–21).

The duties of the watchman were threefold:

1. *To wait and watch for what God would command and warn His people;*
2. *To watch over and superintend the people (see also Isa. 56:10);*
3. *To warn the people for God.*

God has given His ministers a grave responsibility, and He will minister to all our needs if we obey Him, keep His Word, and apply it to our lives. The minister, as God's flame of fire, stands with the wicked and righteous men's blood on his hands, if he does not warn them against evil.

This is his potential and experiential position because he can warn men of God's wrath on their fallen state and point them to the salvation of God in Jesus Christ. The minister will certainly face God if he does not sound the trumpet to wicked people and warn them of the consequences of their sins. He will also bow his knees to our Creator and Father God if he does not warn the righteous that they can die in their sins. If they do not repent, their sin cancels their righteousness, and they can go to hell. *Eternal security*, misinterpreted and mislabeled over the years, has caused many children of God to take their position in Christ for granted because they felt that "once saved always saved." However, we should not focus on eternal security but on *security in Christ Jesus.*

Study chapters 3 and 33 of Ezekiel in light of God's revelation and interpretation of these words as they relate to our call to stand in the gap between God and man. As I read and studied these awesome chapters during my years of ministry, God impressed upon me the importance of His calling on my life to deliver the good news of His gospel.

My theology was shaken and redefined by God Himself as I became not just a reader of His Word, not just a pastor who studies the Word for sermon preparation, but a student on God's assigned program. God strengthened my faith and challenged my convictions and beliefs. In fact, God deprogrammed the errors of some of my theology by reprogramming me in the righteousness of His Word.

One of the major doctrines and traditions of men that made the Word of God of no effect in my life was eternal security. Some years ago I began to rethink what God, in Jesus, meant by saying: "But he that shall endure unto the end, the same shall be saved" (Matt. 24:13). Jesus said this repeatedly in the four Gospels. Further study of what the Alpha and Omega, the First and the Last, said to the seven Asian churches in the second and third chapters of Revelation led me to experience insecurity in the phrase "once saved, always saved." Chapter 2, verse 7b states: "To him that overcometh will I give to eat of the tree of life, which is in the midst of the paradise of God." In chapter 3, verse 5, I read that "He that overcometh, the same shall be clothed in white raiment; and I will not blot out his name out of the book of life, but I will confess his name before my father, and before his angels."

Our salvation is in Jesus and obedience to God's word. Therein we are secure. Our security for eternal life lies in Jesus. Therefore, we must keep the Word of God. We must be lifelong learners, and we must apply God's revelation of His written word in our lives. Later, at God's direction, I studied Chapter 33 of Ezekiel. Here I found that, as a responsible preacher and pastor of His people, I could lose my salvation by disobeying God, by not having enough love for God and His people to warn them of God's call from wickedness. I learned that their blood, as well as that of the "good" sister or brother who handsomely supported the church's program in tithes, time, and offerings, would be on my hands. Supporters, although righteous in their living, sometimes need warning and redirection back onto the path of their walk with God. Sometimes they have strayed in their hearts from Christ even though not observably in their public deeds. Whatever the situation, God held and holds me responsible for directing the righteous to continue in their righteousness with Him. Because God changed the doctrine and tradition of men of "once saved, always saved," I am motivated and inspired to make firm my calling in Christ Jesus no matter what I experience in life.

In this highest of all callings on the life of a person, we stand in the gap between God and man in the diverse situations and circumstances of life and death. We stand in the gap between heaven and hell, prosperity and poverty, incorruption and corruption, destruction and construction of lives, abuse by men and use by God, severance and unity of marriages, depression and joy in the Lord, satisfaction of flesh and fulfillment in God's Spirit. Our service in ministry affects the generations to come. Considering our grave responsibility, God molds, shapes, and makes us *His flaming fires.*

In meditating on the power and providence of God's glory, the psalmist said: "Who maketh his angels spirits; his ministers a flaming fire" (Ps. 104:4). This supports the premise of God's ministers standing in the gap between God's people and the dangers and temptations they face. The concept is confirmed in Genesis 3:24: "So he drove out the man; and he placed at the east of the garden of Eden Cherubims, and a flaming sword which turned every way, to keep the way of the tree of life." God placed the *cherubims* and the flaming sword at the east of the garden to prevent sinners from eating of the tree of life and living forever in sin.

Flames of fire lick up all that is about them in battle. Ministers of the gospel are to be in absolute authority, might, and power of God under the anointing of the Holy Spirit. As we preach and teach the full counsel of God, as we operate in the gifts of the Holy

Spirit, as we flow in the Spirit from the living waters within us, we have the delegated power of the Spirit of Christ to heal all manner of sickness and disease and possess all authority over Satan and his demonic angels. Hell is home for Satan and his demons. We must use our authority to cast them out of people and send them back home. The zeal of the Lord should be upon us as we serve others with the Word of God.

Those gospel ministers who assume their God-given power and/or authority can use it to take the cities that they enter into for the glory of God. The counterpart for every action, reaction, or interaction is in the Word. We read in Numbers 22 that Moab was quite aware of Israel's victories and of God being with them in war and in peace. Knowing that God's power was with the children of Israel in warfare, the Moabites feared defeat. They knew that it would take more than natural weapons and man's skill and strength to defeat Israel. Therefore, they enlisted Balaam to pronounce a curse over Israel. The Moabites sought to defeat the Israelites in spiritual warfare so that they would lose the fight in the natural or physical realm. The ultimate plan of Satan is to defeat us in the inner man first so that we will lose whatever he wishes in the natural or physical realm.

If we are already defeated within our minds, our hearts, and our spirits, we have lost the strength to fight with courage, discipline, skill, and fortitude in the natural realm with spiritual weapons. Because this plan succeeds too often, we have not gone forth in the power and authority of God to defeat Satan and his demons in all the ways that God has intended. We must take the ground wherever our foot treads. Done to the glory of God, this will show in the church as well as in our bodies, the temples of God. When Satan's plan succeeds, the result is sickness, disease, wickedness, and the lack of food, shelter, and finances. This occurs often in areas where we lack victory in Christ Jesus.

Sometimes Satan sends persons into the lives of Christians with the intent of breaking their hearts, crushing them, and snuffing out the Word of God, the power of God, the flow of His Spirit and their obedience to the Lord of Glory. Ultimately, Satan seeks to weaken the Christian, to turn him away from the Lord to him. Satan's strategy is to cause the Christian to enter into a lifestyle of sin and habits that would damn his soul. We have to maintain self-confidence and faith in God during this time; heartbreak comes to take away our self-confidence. We have to maintain our courage during this time by submerging ourselves in God's Word; it will encourage us in the Lord. We have to be strong in the Lord during heartbreaking and distressing experiences that remove us from self-discipline in obedience to God's Word. The strength in the Lord and in the power of His might is available to us. Jesus, the Whole Armor of God, helps us to stand against the wiles (plans or strategies) of the Devil. We must be aware: "For we wrestle not against flesh and blood, but against principalities, against powers, against the rulers of the darkness of this world, against spiritual wickedness in high places" (Eph. 6:12).

The Spirit of the Lord was upon Jesus when He said: "Because he hath anointed me to preach the gospel to the poor; he hath sent me to heal the brokenhearted, to preach deliverance to the captives, and recovering of sight to the blind, to set at liberty them that are bruised, To preach the acceptable year of the Lord" (Luke 4:18–19). The Spirit must be upon us so that we may do His will. Ministers who are flames of fire are careful to do things God's way so that they will receive God's ultimate and greater blessings. We must learn to be sensitive to God's Spirit in order to please and obey Him. God gets pleasure from our obedience to Him.

Miriam, Aaron, and Moses were surely flames of fire before God. They traveled with the tribes of Israel out of Egypt and into the wilderness; however, God prevented each of them from going into the Promised Land because of their individual acts of disobedience to God. We, too, must be careful not to miss God and His ultimate, greater blessing(s) upon us because of acts of rebellion. To obey is better than to sacrifice; to hearken is better than the fat of rams.

Only through the strength of God's Spirit can we conquer and take the land. The strength for any miraculous work of man comes from God's Spirit. "Not by might, nor by power, but by my Spirit, saith the LORD of hosts" (Zech. 4:6).

Israel learned this, as we read in Numbers 21:1–3:

> And when king Arad the Canaanite, which dwelt in the south, heard tell that Israel came by way of the spies; then he fought against Israel, and took some of them prisoners. And Israel vowed a vow unto the LORD, and said, "If thou wilt indeed deliver this people into my hand, then I will utterly destroy their cities." And the LORD hearkened to the voice of Israel, and delivered up the Canaanites; and they utterly destroyed them and their cities: and he called the name of the place Hormah.

How mistaken we are sometimes in our own self-confidence! We attempt to succeed in great undertakings in our private lives, in our families, on the job, and in ministries without God's strength through Jesus Christ. Our success lies in our faith in Him. Jesus gives us the strength to endure the difficulties in life. This is His blessing to us. The Anointing to do great exploits for God resides in Him, not us. *Great exploits are about Him, not us.*

If we are going to be the flames of fire He chooses to work through, we must position ourselves to be available and accessible to Jesus Christ and God, our Father. It is not enough, however, to be available and accessible. We must yield to His calling us to achieve any task, to move when He demands, to hear His voice and unction in our hearts. We are His. We go where He tells us to go and do what He tells us to do. How can we do this? By having the faith in Christ Jesus that gives us the self-confidence to know that "I can do all things through Christ which strengtheneth me" (Phil. 4:13).

What are these *things*? These are the assignments that God gives to us and calls us to do in Him and for Him. When we walk in our assignment, we have faith in God and confidence in ourselves. We receive the energy to do His biddings. When we yield ourselves to His will and are assured by Him that this is our way because it is His way, we walk, talk, pray, praise, and worship by faith and not by sight. When God assures us that we are doing His will according to His Word, the impossible becomes possible. Our way is clear. Our goals are sure, and we run toward our vision. We write the vision, and we read it. We run toward it, and we have patience in the Lord to bring it to pass.

Some will say that we are cocky and arrogant. How mistaken they are! We exhibit self-confidence because of our faith in Jesus who saved us. We are self-confident because of God, our Father, who called us. We are self-confident because of our belief that the Holy Spirit leads, guides, and directs us. We know that the Holy Spirit is helping us because our task is of Him and not ourselves. Therefore, no matter what gets in the way of completing the assignment, we are more than conquerors through Him who strengthens us. We know that we can overcome any obstacle that the Enemy, Satan, puts in our way because the road is clear; out of darkness has come light. The burden is easier to carry because Jesus helps us to carry His yoke, and our *rest* is in Him. Because of the vision in our hearts, temporary problems are just that, solvable problems. Because of the vision, difficulties are just difficulties to be worked out, to overcome, to live through because we know Him who helps us to grow through any circumstances in life. When we look beyond the obstacles, when we look beyond the difficulties, when we look beyond the spiritual warfare to the vision, every problem is solvable because we work toward *God's vision in us*.

Some people might question the assertion that it is God's vision in us, but we know that the Word is *God's vision in us!* James 1:17 states: "*Every* good gift and every perfect gift is from above, and cometh down *from* the Father of lights, with whom is no variableness, neither shadow of turning." If the vision that you and I possess as flames of fire is truly a God-given vision, then we must not beat our chests or expend energy on another vision that we choose. If it is not God-given or God-led, it is of us and not of God. Therefore, God does not sanction the energy, talent, gifts, and resources needed to accomplish the vision. If the vision is of God, however, it is a good and perfect gift from Our Father of lights. It is achievable because Father God equips us to accomplish His assignments. *He gives a vision that we have the potential to achieve.* He equips us with the provision for the vision. He does not frustrate His children, nor does He waste their time or talents. He builds up His own.

God's vision becomes our vision because He divinely instills it in our hearts and our spirits; He impresses it upon our minds. When God leads us, it is possible to know what God wants us to do. When we are not working toward it, we feel guilty or frustrated because we must work toward our assignment, the God-given vision. God's vision for us becomes our vision because we know that it is of Him. We receive it as our own. We embrace it as our possession because we know from whom it came. Therefore, God gives us the wisdom to know that we must believe in Him. He gives us the knowledge that we must trust Him absolutely and depend on Him to bring forth the vision through us.

As flames of fire, we must trust God to shape, mold, and develop us into the person He needs to achieve the vision as He sees it. We often overlook the role of faith in and dependence on God in our spiritual lives. I cite here Jeremiah 18:1–4:

> The *word* which came to Jeremiah from the LORD, saying, "Arise, and go down to the potter's house, and there I will cause thee to hear my words." Then I went down to the potter's house, and behold, he wrought a work on the wheels. And the vessel that he made of clay was marred in the hand of the potter: so he made it again another vessel as seemed good to the potter to make it.

God revealed the plan for His beloved nation, Israel, to Jeremiah. The Israelites were God's Chosen People even as we are God's chosen ministers. The Godhead wanted the best for

Israel as He wants the best for us, and the condition for receiving the best for their lives, and for ours, is repentance from sin and evil and obedience to God's word. God knew that repentance from evil would prevent sudden destruction from their enemy, but the Israelites disobeyed as depicted in Jeremiah 18:12: "And they said, 'There is no hope: but we will walk after our own devices, and we will every one do the imagination of his evil heart.'" For this lapse in judgment, for this sin, God allowed the Babylonians to destroy their cities and lead them into captivity. Their captors jeered, and the Israelites didn't sing Zion's songs in a strange land.

Let us look at these Scriptures in relation to ourselves as His flames of fire and as potential flames of fire. Jeremiah's revelation from God certainly relates to us. First, we are the clay in the Master Potter's hands, God's hands. He's the Potter. We are the clay. As I understand this vivid example, the Potter, God, has the right to deal with a sinful being according to His own counsel or will. The Potter sets out to make us into the vessel He requires in order for us to perform as He desires. Sometimes, however, as sinful beings with a tendency toward the world, the flesh, and the Devil, we sin. We are marred in the Potter's hand, and He is displeased with us. Therefore, He providentially allows us to suffer the consequences of our action and be broken. When we stray from the loving hands of God, we become contrite and brokenhearted. When we are sorrowful for our sins of commission and omission, we repent and turn back to God. Because He loves us even when we are sinful, He watches over us and lovingly cares for those who have lost their way.

When we repent, we come back to Him in obedience to His will. He picks us, "the broken clay," up and begins His work again in us. "So he made it again another vessel, as seemed good to the potter to make it." Often we are not ready to achieve the vision, or certain parts of it, until God breaks us. He prunes us of sin before we are ready for the Master's use. He wants pure, beautiful vessels, showing forth His glory and power, to use as instruments of His love; peace; and power to heal, save, deliver, and build His church.

It is God, through us, who builds the house. It is God, through us, who keeps watch over the city. "Except the LORD build the house, they labour in vain that build it: except the LORD keep the city, the watchman waketh but in vain" (Ps. 127:1). We must trust and reverence the Lord to develop and process us into the anointed ones He requires to achieve His purposes and plans on the earth. When we yield ourselves to Him in faith, He increases His anointing on us, and our anointing becomes stronger.

Secondly, to achieve what God wants to do in our lives, we must depend on Him to lead. After all, it is His vision. Proverbs 20:24 says, "Man's goings are of the LORD; how can a man understand his own way?" *The Living Bible* states: "Since the Lord is directing our steps, why try to understand everything that happens along the way?"

May I pause here, my Christian friends, and speak to those of us who have a strong tendency to analyze every major occurrence that we experience in our Christian ministry and walk with God. This tendency is a strength that can become a weakness and a hindrance. Strength allows us to learn from our experiences; however, it is a hindrance when we perceive that God wants us to move, and we do not respond. For if we do not move with the leading and flow of the Holy Spirit, we hinder and delay the move of God's hand in our lives. We are stuck where we are in our own knowledge. We are wasting our intelligence, energy, talents, gifts, and resources endeavoring to understand beyond our human capacity. That which is beyond our understanding is in God's hands, and we have to trust Him.

When we do not trust God to lead us, we often experience unexpected and incomprehensible delays. This has been one of my greatest weaknesses—not trusting God absolutely. When I came to the shocking realization that only I—not circumstances, not someone else, not God—was delaying me, I had to find a way to overcome this fault. How comforting to realize that God directs my steps even in the things that absolutely mystify me. Yet, those were the very areas in which I needed to trust and depend on Him. This realization delivered me from confusion and relieved my frustrations. I ceased worrying when I stopped being overly analytical. During Bible study, I read Proverbs 20:24 in The Living Bible (TLB). "Since the Lord is directing our steps, why try to understand everything that happens along the way?" and Proverbs 16:9: "A man's heart deviseth his way: but *the LORD directeth his steps.*" God also led me to Psalm 37:23a (TLB), "The steps of good men are directed by the Lord. He delights in each step they take."

These verses brought relief. I gave up my attempts to understand what God was doing in my life. After becoming a child of God at age nineteen, my ultimate desire was to follow the Lord and be consecrated to Him. If I were going to trust Him for His power and anointing in my life, I would have to depend on Him for His leading, guiding, and directing me. My life would have to be given to Him completely.

When I had a collision with a train at an intersection, was pulled down the railroad tracks for seventy-one feet, and survived with only a few bruises, cuts, and a contusion of the knee, I knew afterwards that He supernaturally *protects, guides, and leads me.* My ultimate dependence is on Him. He can do as He chooses in my life. Again, I made a choice to follow Him wherever He leads.

Several stark realities confronted me. First, I could have lost arms, legs, or even my head in the accident. I could have lost my life instantly. Secondly, I began to thank and praise God for the major functions of my body that we often took for granted. Thirdly, I thanked Him for the ability to walk, talk, to have the function of my limbs. I might have been paralyzed for life or lost the ability to chew food. Moreover, I concluded that when a minister serves Christ and God under the anointing of His Spirit, God keeps him alive to fulfill his calling and assignment. In God's timing, I was not destined to die until my assignment had been accomplished! Because of that accident, however, I trust God more deeply to complete His work in and through me.

I know that the body is just the shell that houses the soul and spirit and that all God has materially given to me—house, clothes, car, job, and food—is to sustain the body. Yet, the work of God within my mind, soul, and spirit is the most important aspect of my life. My supreme task is to allow Him, by faith, to minister through me as I make myself available and accessible to Him. As one of His potential flames of fire, I realize that it is all about *HIM*, not me or us. Life is all about what He chooses to do in our lives.

In consideration of what He chooses to do in my life, I know that if I fulfill God's will according to His Word, He will provide for me abundantly. This abundance will be more than I could ask or think. Please understand that God assumes full responsibility for calling us to the ministry. He provides adequately for us as we fulfill His mission and purposes and obey the mandates in His Divine Word. Our responsibility is to fulfill His calling on our lives. Just remember that those whom He calls, He equips to succeed.

CHAPTER 9

THE MINISTER'S PROVISION

Grace and peace be multiplied unto you through the knowledge of our God, and of Jesus our Lord. According as his divine power hath given unto us all things that pertain unto life and godliness, through the knowledge of him that hath called us to glory and virtue: Whereby are given unto us exceeding great and precious promises: that by these ye might be partakers of the divine nature, having escaped the corruption that is in the world through lust.

—2 Peter 1:2–4

O ur knowledge and God's power are the field of our strength according to our faith in God for our daily spiritual and material provision. We understand and know in our hearts and spirits that God will supply all our needs according to His riches in glory by Christ Jesus. God only is our source of every good and perfect gift from the Father of Lights.

As long as Satan can keep us striving for our daily provision of shelter, food, clothes, and adequate monies to pay our bills while we live above our financial means, we are in bondage. We must destroy this yoke by the Holy Spirit's power, the anointing. Satan and his demons scheme to keep our focus off God and the things that pertain to spiritual life. Satan knows that as long as we are busy and unfocused, we are off center with God. Therefore, we are less likely to flow in the things of the Spirit of God that would develop us into ministers who are flames of fire.

God wants us free from material wants so that we are at liberty to follow Him into deeper revelations and knowledge of God. God wants us to be more effective and powerful in teaching and ministry. Jesus gave us a stern warning: Man cannot serve two masters; either he will love God and serve Him or love money and be too attached or controlled by it. Jesus wants the leaders of the Christian army to be free from earthly attachments so that we have the flexibility to do as the *General of generals* commands us.

I implore you to understand the central thought conveyed here: We must be concerned about adequate substance for our personal needs and fulfillment. We must be prudent in financial matters or be willing to obtain the knowledge that will make us proficient. We must share God's financial blessings with those to whom we minister. Yet, we must never be slaves to our financial situation. God is *the source of our supply for everything.* Besides, our strength is in God, not in our possessions.

Paul knew these things. In his letter to Timothy, he discusses how a person becomes a good soldier of Jesus Christ. To be a good soldier for Jesus Christ, burning with the zeal of God and baptized in the fire of the Holy Ghost, we must realize that our lives are not in the things we possess. Our lives exist and have their being in the power and strength of God, our Father. Therefore, Paul was correct in his advice to Timothy:

> Thou therefore, my son, be strong in the grace that is in Christ Jesus. And the things that thou hast heard of me among many witnesses, the same commit thou to faithful men, who shall be able to teach others also. Thou therefore *endure hardness,* as a good soldier of Jesus Christ. No man that warreth entangleth himself with the affairs of this life; that he may please him who hath chosen him to be a soldier. And if a man also strive for masteries, yet is he not crowned, *except* he strive lawfully. The husbandman that laboureth must be first partaker of the

fruits. Consider what I say; and the Lord give thee understanding in all things.

—2 Timothy 2:1–7

In short, our greatest strength is in the grace of Jesus Christ.
We must impart the revelatory knowledge that God gives us
to faithful people of God's army so that they may teach others,
also. We should not be afraid of hardness as soldiers of God. We
must endure it to become stronger and better equipped as good
soldiers for our Lord. We must not be slaves to the things of this
life nor allow the affairs of life to choke out or make the grace and
power of God within us ineffective.

In striving to excel in the spirit of excellence, to become a
master in spiritual warfare with absolute power over the authority
of Satan, we must win the battles and the war according to God's
plan for us. We must be strong soldiers (partakers) of the Lord
Jesus to impart this fruit and these experiences into the lives of
others. In our observation and actions, the Lord gives us a greater
understanding of life and of the depth, height, breadth, and
length of the love of Christ Jesus.

Paul does not stop there, however. He had more to say about
attachment to the things of this life, things that are only a means
to the end for our provision. *God is our Source* for provisions.

Nevertheless the foundation of God standeth sure, having this
seal, the Lord knoweth them that are his. And, let everyone
that nameth the name of Christ depart from iniquity. But in
a great house there are not only vessels of gold and of silver,
but also of wood and of earth; and some to honour, and some
to dishonour. If a man therefore purge himself from these,
he shall be a vessel unto honour, sanctified, and meet for the
master's use, and prepared unto every good work.

—2 Timothy 2:19–21

Financial bondage and attachment to material things are
the reasons that many ministers, who are Spirit filled, find it
difficult to break away from the churches' traditions. Churches

sometimes have an unspoken and unwritten policy that holds the minister in financial bondage.

If he really moves in the gifts of the Holy Spirit and obeys God instead of observing the closely held policy, the minister is threatened with dismissal. The "elders" communicate their displeasure in subtle ways to "keep the minister in line" with commonly accepted and long-standing traditions. This should not be! God wants to show His glory and power in all denominational churches, among all races, religions, creeds, and cultures. God desires to move Christians away from the ways of man to the ways of God. God wants to inspire saints to think on higher levels according to His thoughts and away from the doctrines of man that make the things of God of no effect. God said, "For my thoughts are not your thoughts, neither are your ways my ways, saith the LORD. For as the heavens are higher than the earth, so are my ways higher than your ways, and my thoughts than your thoughts" (Isa. 55:8–9).

God wants His ministers who would be flames of fire to move in the things of God. Jesus died so that we would be saved, redeemed from the curses of men; God sits on the throne and uses any means necessary to get us to see His goodness and merciful desire to lead us "beside the still waters." The Holy Spirit of our Living God is doing His work on earth. He seeks the man or woman whose heart is perfect toward Him, fully dedicated to His service to do His work on earth. The Holy Spirit desires people who will toil in the vineyard without hesitation or reservation, not shrinking from any area of God's calling on their lives. He is looking for Christians to stand in the gap between heaven and hell, God and man, life and death, prosperity and poverty, corruption and incorruption, for individual souls and their spiritual welfare. God seeks a people who will stand before Him, uncompromisingly, with faith in Him, to please Him and believe that He will provide for their every need.

God's foundation is Christ, and He builds saints on that foundation. Christ knows each of us by name. He admonishes

Christians to divorce themselves from the earthly attachments, possessions, or relationships that encumber and prevent us from moving in the anointing of God to achieve His purpose in us. We must be aware that money is only the means to an end for our welfare. We need it in sufficient amounts to accomplish the purpose of spreading the gospel of the Kingdom to the ends of the earth.

Yet we must never *love* money; *the love of money* can cause us to err from the faith and to pierce ourselves through with many sorrows. Dependence on money to solve our problems weakens our dependency in our true Source, God. Total dependence on God extricates us from the possession of things to be God's ministers of fire. When preached with the Fire of the Holy Ghost, the gospel of Jesus Christ burns the sin from man's heart and life, brings him to the saving power of God unto salvation, and develops him into the pure vessel that is ready for our Master's use.

Our Father God, Jehovah Jireh, wants abundantly prosperous children. We are heirs and joint heirs with Christ our Lord. We are priests and kings under our great High Priest and King of Glory, Jesus Christ. And Christ's Word, the Bible, tells us that He inspired John to write for our comfort and assurance that God wants us to be spiritually, emotionally, and physically prosperous. A sound mind in a sound body is the principle. "Beloved, *I wish above all things that* thou mayest prosper and be in health, *even as* thy soul prospereth" (3 John 1:2). "But seek ye first the kingdom of God, and his righteousness; and *all these things* shall be added unto you" (Matt. 6:33). If we consistently seek God's face first and His righteousness, as the deer pants after the water, God will bless us with His exceedingly abundant blessings above all we can think or ask.

Faith in God pleases Him and is required for complete dependence on Him for our welfare and ministerial needs. Dependence on God affects our decisions and associations. The Word warns us to shun persons who use profanity and those who are vain because the association can cause us to incorporate the same actions and attitudes into our own lives. We can maintain our position in Christ, our Foundation, as God's watchmen without coming down off the wall to mingle with corrupt associates. God called us to minister to all people; yet we must not be involved in their evil devices. He called us to be His flames of fire; we must not allow the polluted sins of the world to extinguish our flame. God wants to cleanse us thoroughly from vainness, profanity, and the influences of the luxuries of men. God purposes to purge us from these things in order to develop us into vessels of honor, sanctified and prepared unto every good work. He wants us meet for the Master's use.

God does not overlook our need for sustenance. His Word promises abundance for His children. When the church of the Living God comes into God's revelation of the Scriptures, we will experience the abundant blessings of God. The world is rich in goods controlled by Satan and his forces of evil. They do everything that they can to keep us from experiencing the blessings of God. Satan knows that when the church of God comes into *the full counsel of God*, it will begin to receive the blessings of God; His saints will defeat Satan and regain that which he has stolen over the centuries. God will give the wealth of the wicked to His saints to defeat Satan. He wants us to possess the resources to accomplish His purposes on the earth; therefore, Satan works to prevent the blessings of God from coming to His saints.

Satan deceives too many Christians about God's promises of prosperity for His children. This is one of the most elaborate and frequently used schemes of hell. Our task, then, is to promote knowledge in this area to keep the saints from perishing and/ or missing God's abundance. We must let God be true, for "According as his divine power hath given unto us all things that pertain unto life and godliness, through the knowledge of him that hath called us to glory and virtue" (2 Pet. 1:3). We must not be deceived about the abundance that God wants His ministers and the church to possess. Ministers, as flames of fire, must receive the abundance that God offers to achieve His will and build His kingdom on earth.

Some of us are taught to reject God's abundance. Consequently, some of us reject those who have accepted God's abundance. Two of the hardest and most crucial things ministers and pastors deal with are rejection and criticism. This is especially difficult when it comes from well-meaning Christians. Sometimes other ministers are the source of such rejection. People reject ministers for teaching about God's more than sufficient provisions as part of the full counsel of God. We must prepare for such critics who usually lack knowledge of God's promises to His people on this subject. We cannot allow critics to keep us from undertaking the tasks that God has set before us. We must always desire God's favor more than we want man's favor. When we refuse to stand up and be counted, the body of Christ lacks sufficient provisions.

It was an unfortunate experience for me, as a young child, to live in an environment that fostered the sinful, unspoken error that to be poor was to be saintly. That the church often accepted this lie was even more regrettable. It took years of Bible study and fellowship with Jesus for me to erase this false doctrine from my mind and way of living. It is sad to say, but we are still dealing with this false doctrine and tradition. We do not accept the promises of God for prosperity in all areas of our lives, but we should.

Bear with me while I mention a few Scriptures that promise abundant living. "Now unto him that is able to do exceeding abundantly above all that we can ask or think, according to the power that worketh in us" (Eph. 3:20). This verse informs me that, by the power of the Holy Spirit, my Father God is more than capable of responding to my faith in Him as I pray and meditate on His providing for me. In fact, He is more than able to exceed my requests in prayer. God responds and acts on my faith in Him according to His Holy Spirit's power, and I receive more of His anointing as I respond to Him in faith. I acquire more of the Holy Spirit's power as I study and meditate on His

Word, receive it in my mind and heart, and apply it in practical, living experiences. My prayers are answered because God acts on my petitions to Him based on my faith in Him as I pray. It is my faith in Him that moves His blessings toward me. So our prayers must be to God if we desire an answer to our petitions. Moreover, our prayers must be in line with God's Word and His will. "And this is the confidence that we have in him, that, if we ask *any thing* according to his will, he heareth us: *and if* we know that he hear us, *whatsoever* we ask, we know that we have the petitions that we desired of him" (1 John 5:14–15).

Even though we know that Jesus intercedes for us at the right hand of God, if we expect answers to our prayers, our daily living must be in accordance with the will of God also. If we practice a sinful lifestyle, we position ourselves as sinners who do not know the Lord. Therefore, we put up a wall or hindrance to answers to our heartfelt desires.

Another erroneous doctrine in the church is that God, our Father, does not give us our desires. This is not scripturally sound! Psalm 37:4–5 says, "Delight *thyself* also in the LORD; and *he shall* give thee the desires of thine heart. Commit thy way unto the LORD; trust also in him; and he shall bring it to pass." According to God's Word, as we find our delight, our joy, our good pleasure in the Lord, He will give us our desires. God is a God of priorities and order; He fulfills our needs first. Yet, He answers us above that which we can ask or think.

To receive God's exceedingly abundant blessings, we must meet certain conditions. Psalm 37:5 gives the conditions: "Commit thy way unto the LORD; trust also in him, and he shall bring it to pass." If we want God's blessings, we must commit our mind, body, soul, and lifestyle to Him. We must commit our will as children of God unto His divine direction for our lives. We must commit our conduct, our thoughts, and our lives to God. We must make a commitment to be righteous.

The second condition for receiving God's blessings is to trust in Him. We must trust Him as the Father of our provisions. We must trust Him as Jehovah Jireh, the provider of our natural and spiritual needs. We must trust Him to be with us in times of sickness and despair. We must trust Him with our heartache and heartbreaks. We must trust Him to provide a way out when we are tempted. In James 1:12, we learn, "Blessed is the man that endureth temptation: for *when* he is tried, *he shall receive* the crown of life, which the Lord hath promised to them that love him." We must trust Him for comfort and aid when people persecute us because we believe in Him. Notice Jesus' reply to Peter in Mark 10:28–31:

> Then Peter began to say unto him, "Lo, we have left all, and have followed thee." And Jesus answered and said, "Verily I say unto you, there is *no man that hath left* house, or brethren, or sisters, or father, or mother, or wife, or children, or lands, for my sake, and the gospel's, *But he shall receive* an hundredfold now in this time, houses, and brethren, and sisters, and mothers, and children, and lands, with persecutions; and in the world to come eternal life. But many that are first shall be last; and the last first."

Paul supplemented Jesus' statements with further commentary when he wrote, "Yea, and all that will live godly in Christ Jesus shall suffer persecution. But evil men and seducers shall wax worse and worse, deceiving, and being deceived. But *continue thou* in the things which thou has learned and has been assured of, knowing of whom thou has learned them" (2 Tim. 3:12–14).

There is a direct relationship between the kind of life we live and the power of God in us to do the works of Christ, the hope of glory. The psalmist tells us what is required of potential flames of fire:

> *Who* shall ascend into the hill of LORD? or *who* shall stand in his holy place? *He that* hath clean hands, and a pure heart; who hath not lifted up his soul unto vanity, nor sworn deceitfully. *He shall* receive the blessing from the LORD, and righteousness from the God of his salvation. This is

the generation of them that seek him, that seek thy face, O Jacob. Selah.

—Psalm 24:3–6

God requires clean hands, pure hearts, forgiveness, mercy, and truth. He demands humility, trust, and reverence. He expects consistent praise. According to James 3:9–12, we should use the tongue to encourage rather than discourage our fellow man:

> Therewith bless we God, even the Father; and therewith curse we men, which are made after the similitude of God. Out of the same mouth proceedeth blessing and cursing. My brethren, these things ought not so to be. Doth a fountain send forth at the same place sweet water and bitter? Can the fig tree, my brethren, bear olive berries? Either a vine, figs? So can no fountain both yield salt water and fresh.

If we are flames of fire with and for the Lord, our inward character must be pure. If we are going to spread God's word by teaching, preaching, and prophesying with the fire of the Holy Spirit, our character must be clean for the greatest effective use by our Savior, Jesus Christ.

Today, we hear very little about godliness or godly living in the church. Devotion to Christ, God, and the Holy Spirit appears to have been pushed aside or forgotten. This is what Psalm 37:4–5 intended as the way of trusting, delighting in the Lord, and committing of our way unto Him. Piety as a devoted life and lifestyle appears to have little significance in the lives of today's Christians. Yet, if our wicked world is to experience real, widespread revival, we must return to God in our personal lives. For even as judgment must begin in the house of God, so real revival must begin in the body of Jesus Christ, the church.

God provides abundantly for our spiritual needs so that we can do great exploits for Him, so that we are signs and wonders of Him on the earth. We do not seek God's face only for His blessings; we seek God's face to be in His presence. We seek God's face to experience the joy of the Lord as our strength. We seek God's face to know Him on the most intimate level. We seek God's face to offer Him thanksgiving. We seek His face to praise Him. We seek God's face to love Him and to embrace His will. We seek God's face to become His friend and not just His servant. We seek God's face to abide in Him and to grow in Him because we know that, without Him, we cannot be effective. We seek His face to experience the glory, the presence of the Lord. We seek His face to experience the Fire of the Holy Spirit. We seek His face to so be filled and baptized in His power that as we lift Jesus up, man will be drawn to Him and be saved. We seek Jesus' face, God's face, the presence of the Holy Spirit so that as we minister, God is really ministering the melodious gospel of Jesus through us, His instruments. We want to be in the presence of God, our Consuming Fire, and survive. If we survive His fiery presence, we become ministers—flames of fire. We shall have been in the furnace of His essence. The fire of His being is on and in us. Therefore, we serve Him and others with the fire of the Holy Spirit that saves, delivers, liberates, heals, and makes men whole.

Our dependence on God develops us into the flames of fire that He wants us to be. I note here a very familiar Scripture passage to deal with this important issue:

> The word which came to Jeremiah from the LORD saying, "Arise, and go down to the potter's house, and there I will cause thee to hear my words." Then I went down to the potter's house, and, behold, he wrought a work on the wheels. And the vessel that he made of clay was marred in the hand of the potter: so he made it again another vessel, as seemed good to the potter to make it. Then the word of the LORD came to me, saying, "O house of Israel, cannot I do with you as this potter?" saith the LORD. "Behold, as the clay is in the potter's hand, so are ye in mine hand, O house of Israel. At what instant I shall speak concerning a nation and concerning a kingdom, to pluck up, and to pull down, and to destroy it; if that nation, against whom I have pronounced, turn from their evil, I will repent of the evil that I thought to do unto them. And at what instant I shall speak concerning

a nation and concerning a kingdom, to build and to plant it; if it do evil in my sight, that it obey not my voice, then I will repent of the good, wherewith I said I would benefit them. Now therefore go to, speak to the men of Judah, and to the inhabitants of Jerusalem, saying, '*Thus saith the LORD*; Behold, I frame evil against you, and devise a device against you: return ye now every one from his evil way, and make your ways and your doings good.'" And they said, "There is no hope: but we will walk after our own devices, and we will every one do the imagination of his evil heart."

—Jeremiah 18:1–12

The Jews, whom God designated as His chosen people, lived in Judah and Jerusalem. Today, God's ministers spread the glorious message of His Word throughout the earth. Our preaching, teaching, and sharing methodology is closely related to how well we have yielded our will to God.

Jeremiah received a directive from the mighty voice of God to go down to the potter's house to receive the revelatory will of God by observing a master craftsman, the potter, at work on his wheel and by hearing the Word of God. The potter was focused, absolutely involved in his trade. Just as the potter creates his chosen vessel or object, so God develops us into the flames of fire He desires. Often this is contrary to our wills, our desires, and our selfish whims; we prefer to achieve success, prosperity, and influence according to man's way rather than God's way. Paul addresses these issues in his statement about God's provision for our needs according to His riches in glory by Christ Jesus.

So Jeremiah observes the potter at work with a vessel in his hand. "And the vessel that he made of clay was marred in the hand of the potter: so he made it again another vessel, as seemed good to the potter to make it" (Jer. 18:4). When a vessel was marred, it was not thrown away; the clay was crushed together and returned to the wheel, and the work began again. This continued until the clay took on the shape the potter intended. This is what God declared He would do with Israel.

This is what happens to ministers called of God at some time during their lives. After receiving the call to the ministry, we start out on fire for God as one of his vessels, but something "mars" us in God's hand. He is unable to bring the work He has begun in us to completion. The marring might have been caused by a weakness, some character flaw or a situation beyond our control. We may have sinned and not asked for forgiveness. Whatever the situation or reason, God loves us, and He has compassion on those whom He has called. Therefore, He picks up our broken, crushed pieces to refine us into the vessel He first intended.

The emphasis is on God's intention, His purpose, His plan, not ours. Yet, while we were perhaps enjoying our fallen state, some of us might have become stiff-necked, like the Israelites, and too stubborn to yield again to the Master Potter's hands. Their reply to God's stern warning through Jeremiah in verses 11–12 was nothing short of spiritual suicide:

> "Now therefore go to, speak to the men of Judah, and to the inhabitants of Jerusalem, saying, '*Thus saith the LORD*: Behold I frame evil against you, and devise a device against you: return ye now every one from his evil way, and make your ways and your doings good.'" And they said, "There is no hope: but we will walk after our own devices, and we will every one do the imagination of his evil heart."

Does this speak to you as a potential flame of fire? God planned for the Babylonians to descend from the north upon Israel as a hot boiling cauldron poured out upon the nation to destroy it. Their reply was the stubbornness of sinful hearts. The Bible proclaims, in Proverbs 29:1, "He, that being often reproved hardeneth his neck, shall suddenly be destroyed, and that without remedy." There is always hope in Jesus if we choose to ask for forgiveness of our sin(s): For He is our hope of glory. If you yearn for sweet peace and you have not found it, yield your body, your soul, your mind, and your spirit to God the Father.

The potter's clay, though marred in his hands, was still malleable. It was sensitive to the craftsman's touch. It was pliable enough to yield to his hands. If we would be the willing vessels through which God does His greatest, most authoritative work, we, too, have to be sensitive to the Father's touch, desires, and decisions.

There are a number of pine trees in my back yard and my neighbor's yard. Sometimes, when the wind blows before a storm, the trees bend and sway in powerful strength of the wind. The whistling sound that they make is eerie, but since they yield to nature's power, they withstand terrible storms. Their firm roots allow them to bend to the forces of nature rather than break. We, too, must bend, sway, and yield to the moving wind of God's Spirit.

Our loving, compassionate, merciful, and gracious Father God wants us to be flexible in His hands. He is the Potter; we are the clay. He wants to pick us up in His loving, skillful hands and mold us into the most compassionate and loving flames of fire on this earth. He wants to develop us into the most powerful flames of fire the world has ever experienced, but we have to yield to Him, fully surrendering to the will of His Word, fully surrendering to the unction of the Holy Spirit in our hearts. This is the provision of development God wants to bring into our lives.

God intends that no obedient flame of fire lack sufficient and abundant provision in this life. He wants us to be free from material and financial bondage so that we can focus on kingdom building. A "hungry" soldier focuses on his basic needs and material possessions. If he is free of these shackles, however, he is ready for "boot camp" in God's military-spiritual forces. He is prepared, equipped, and ready to become a good warrior for God. He is prepared for the Master's use in spiritual warfare for those to whom he ministers.

CHAPTER 10

A WARRIOR IN SPIRITUAL WARFARE

Finally, my brethren, be strong in the Lord, and in the power of his might. Put on the whole armour of God, that ye may be able to stand against the wiles of the devil. For we wrestle not against flesh and blood, but against principalities, against powers, against the rulers of the darkness of this world, against spiritual wickedness in high places.

—Ephesians 6:10–12

Any one of us whom God called into an office of the fivefold ministry of apostle, prophet, evangelist, pastor, or teacher and who aspires to become a flaming fire for Jesus Christ would do well to realize that we are consistently, and persistently, in spiritual warfare. Spiritual warfare affects our lives and our ministries. Our defeat or victory depends upon our knowledge and skill in using defensive and offensive spiritual weaponry. Knowing that demonic and angelic forces affect the spiritual and natural results in our lives is extremely important and necessitates our putting on "the whole amour of God."

When the opposing forces of Satan's assigned demons attack us, we must be aware that God gave Jesus a name above any principality, power, might, or dominion. When we were born again and adopted into God's family, we inherited the power to defeat Satan and his demons.

> And what is the exceeding greatness of his power to us-ward who believe, according to the working of his mighty power, which he wrought in Christ, when he raised him from the dead, and set him at own right hand in the heavenly places, far above all principality, and power, and might, and dominion, and every name that is named, not only in this world, but also in that which is to come.
>
> —Ephesians 1:19–21

We must not target an institution, organization, or human being when we come under attack. We must focus on and aim our spiritual weapons at the forces of the evil motivators behind the visible enemy. We wrestle not against flesh and blood but against the echelons of Satan. Therefore, it is imperative that we do not delay putting on the whole armor of God. The defensive armor is mainly for protecting us from an attack, so we stand in place or are not pushed back from our God-assigned position. We in Christendom must begin to use God's offensive weapons in the attack against Satan and his forces if we plan to win the battle for spiritual life or death. In other words, we must attack Satan and his forces.

Our spiritual vitality and that of those we serve depend upon our realizing that we have more weapons that are offensive at our disposal than defensive ones. "(For the weapons of our *warfare* are not carnal, but mighty through God to the *pulling down* of strong holds;) *casting down imaginations*, and every high thing that exalteth itself against the knowledge of God, and bringing into captivity every thought to the obedience of Christ" (2 Cor. 10:4–5).

Wear the shield of faith, for without faith all weapons are ineffective. This shield deflects the Enemy's attacks. Jesus used the offensive weapon of God's Word against Satan in the wilderness. Preparation in prayer supports both defensive and offensive weapons: "Praying always with prayer and supplication in the Spirit, and watching thereunto with all perseverance and supplication for all saints" (Eph. 6:18).

We must teach the children of God to defeat Satan during our sojourn here on earth. A list of essential weapons, gifts, and ministries for us to use follows:

THE ARMOR OF GOD

Defensive Weapons (Eph. 6:13–18):

1. Girdle of truth
2. Breastplate of righteousness
3. Preparation of gospel of peace
4. Shield of faith
5. Helmet of salvation
6. Sword of Spirit—Word of God
7. Persistent prayer with perseverance and supplication for all saints

Offensive Weapons:

1. Sword of Spirit—God's Word (Eph. 6:17)
2. Prayer with perseverance for all saints for provisions spiritually and naturally (Eph. 6:18)
3. Praise and worship (Ps. 100:1–5)
4. Pulling down strongholds (2 Cor. 10:4)
5. Casting down sinful imaginations (2 Cor. 10:5)
6. Captivity of every thought to obedience of Christ (2 Cor. 10:5)
7. Liberty in Jesus Christ (Gal. 5:16)
8. Sensitivity to walking in the Spirit (Gal. 5:16)
9. Leading of the Spirit (Gal. 5:18)
10. Strength in the grace of Christ Jesus (2 Tim. 2:1)
11. Spirit of power (2 Tim. 1:7)
12. Spirit of love (2 Tim. 1:7)
13. Spirit of sound mind (2 Tim. 1:7)

14. Walking in the light of Christ (1 John 1:7)
15. Fellowship with other saints (1 John 1:7)
16. Blood of Jesus Christ (1 John 1:7)
17. Intimate fellowship with Christ (1 John 1:6)
18. Confession of sin (1 John 1:9)
19. Faithfulness of Christ (1 John 1:9)
20. Forgiveness of sin (1 John 1:9)
21. Cleansing from unrighteousness (1 John 1:9)
22. Confession of Jesus as Lord by the Holy Ghost (1 Cor. 12:3)

Gifts of Holy Spirit (1 Cor. 12:8–10):

1. Word of wisdom
2. Word of knowledge
3. Gift of faith
4. Gifts of healing
5. Working miracles
6. Gift of prophecy
7. Discerning of spirits
8. Divers kinds of tongues
9. Interpretation of tongues
10. Working of Holy Spirit within us (1 Cor. 12:11)
11. Baptism in Holy Spirit (1 Cor. 12:13)
12. Spirit of wisdom of Christ (Eph. 1:17)
13. Spirit of knowledge of Christ (Eph. 1:17)
14. Hope of Christ's calling us (Eph. 1:18)
15. Eyes of understanding for enlightenment of our spirit (Eph. 1:18)
16. Inherited riches of Christ's glory (Eph. 1:18)
17. Exceeding greatness of Christ's power within us (Eph. 1:19)
18. Working of His mighty power within us (Eph. 1:19)
19. Resurrection of Jesus Christ (Eph. 1:20)
20. Maturing of saints (Eph. 4:12)

21. Work of ministry (Eph. 4:12)
22. Edification of body of Christ (Eph. 4:12)
23. Unity of our faith (Eph. 4:13)
24. Knowledge of God's Son Jesus (Eph. 4:13)
25. Stability of doctrine (Eph. 4:14)
26. Speaking truth in love (Eph. 4:15)
27. Growing in Christ Jesus (Eph. 4:15)
28. Body of Christ fitly joined together (Eph. 4:16)

Fivefold Ministries Given to the Church (Eph. 4:11):

1. Apostles
2. Prophets
3. Evangelists
4. Pastors
5. Teachers

These ministries are to be used for perfecting saints, for work of ministry, for edifying body of Christ. Overall purpose: equipping saints for warfare.

Fruit of the Spirit (Gal. 5:22–23):

1. Fruit of love
2. Fruit of joy
3. Fruit of peace
4. Fruit of longsuffering
5. Fruit of gentleness
6. Fruit of goodness
7. Fruit of faith
8. Fruit of meekness
9. Fruit of temperance (self-control)
10. Knowing power of Christ's resurrection (Phil. 3:10)
11. Knowledge of fellowship of Christ's suffering (Phil. 3:10)

12. Conforming to Christ—dying to self and flesh (Phil. 3:10)
13. Pressing toward prize of high calling of God in Christ Jesus (Phil. 3:14)
14. Praying in the Holy Ghost (Jude 1:20)
15. Angels—our ministering spirits (Heb. 1:14)
16. Power of attorney over Satan in Jesus' name (Luke 10:17)
17. Prayer and fasting (Mark 9:28–29)
18. Binding and loosing (Matt. 16:19)
19. Casting out demons (Mark 16:17)
20. Promises of prosperity (Deut. 28:1–13)
21. Overcoming Satan by the blood of the Lamb and word of our testimony (Rev. 12:11)
22. Power of Christ's resurrection (Phil. 3:10)
23. Mind of Christ (Phil. 2:5–8)

These extensive lists confirm that the offensive weapons for God's flaming fires, as well as other believers, are more in number than the defensive weapons, and this is not an exhaustive list of the weapons listed in both the Old and New Testaments. It is time that we, the ministers of Christ, yield ourselves as vessels of the Anointed One to prepare the church to respond to the attacks and to attack the forces of Satan on earth. We need to attack the devices of evil—drugs, prostitution, homosexuality, corruption in politics, child abuse, wife and husband abuse, abortion, as well as the occult and witchcraft.

While we need the support of the government and our civic leaders, they do not have the answer to society's ills. The secular educational and social institutions do not possess the answer to our world's corruption. Social service agencies need our support, but they treat only the body and mind, not the heart. The answer to our problems lies in the living and true church of God. The answer is in *Jesus*. He alone can change the corrupt to righteousness, holiness, and integrity in Himself. He alone can save the sin-sick soul and make us whole.

Elijah, a flaming fire of God, fought one of the greatest battles known to man when he opposed Baal's 450 prophets. Intensely aware of God's anointing on him, Elijah mounted a bold, aggressive attack against King Ahab, Queen Jezebel, and the false god, Baal. Four hundred fifty false prophets led the nation of Israel in idol worship. Elijah knew that this "call to arms" against Baal's prophets was really a spiritual war against Satan himself. He was not deceived into thinking that he was wrestling against flesh and blood. He was aware that he was in a spiritual war against principalities, powers, rulers of darkness of the world, and spiritual wickedness in high places. This was no time to fear or doubt God. Nothing was more important than to *trust God* to prove Himself as the One God of heaven and earth with the Fire of God from heaven.

This man, a flaming fire of God, did not wait for Satan to attack him and then defend his position. He took the battle to Satan. Elijah set an example for us, the ministers of God and the present day church. We generally get our wake up call at the hand of Satan after he has attacked us. Then we put on our defensive armor and take up our offensive spiritual weapons to fight back. When we do this, we are often already wounded because we have not been "sober, alert and vigilant" toward our adversary who walks about with a lion's roar to frighten and intimidate us so that we shirk from battle. We need to remember that the roar of the lion has never hurt anyone. The sound deceives us into thinking that Satan is more powerful than he really is.

The adversary knows that as long as we are afraid of his growl, we will be less effective than we need to be. He also knows that we have the power of Jesus' name, prayer, the Word of God, the sword of the Spirit, and the believer's authority with which to defeat him. Therefore, it is far better for Satan if we are unaware of our absolute authority over him in Jesus Christ and the Holy Spirit. We, like Elijah, must take the battle to the false prophets and to Satan. God's army, His flames of fire, and the people we lead, must be on the offensive against Satan and his echelon of powers. We must do this to claim the victory and to "possess the land," thus taking back what Satan has stolen from us.

Elijah's faith in God and in himself as an instrument of the one true and living God is evident in 1 Kings 18:21–24:

> And Elijah came unto all the people, and said, "How long halt ye between two opinions? If the LORD be God, then follow him: but if Baal, then follow him." And the people answered him not a word. Then said Elijah unto the people, "I, even I only, remain a prophet of the LORD; but Baal's prophets are four hundred and fifty men. Let them therefore give us two bullocks; and let them choose one bullock for themselves, and cut it in pieces, and lay it on wood, and put no fire under: and I will dress the other bullock, and lay it on wood and put no fire under: And call ye on the name of your gods, and I will call on the name of the LORD; and the God that answereth by *fire*, let him be God." And all the people answered and said, "It is well spoken."

It may appear that Elijah is taking a bold risk, but it was no risk at all. He knew the one and only God from experiencing His miraculous power in the past. Therefore, he offered a challenge to Baal's well-known false prophets in faith. He knew that when God answered by fire from heaven, the people, Israel, would once again see God prove Himself as the only living God, working through Elijah, a channel of His power. The risk appeared great to the spiritually uninitiated, but Elijah was confident.

Once when I was ministering in a New Year's Eve service after preaching, I asked the pastor for coverings for the ladies, as God would minister to them through me and provide healing and deliverance. The Holy Spirit's power manifested itself greatly during that service. Later, the pastor called and asked, "How did you know the people would be overcome by God's Spirit?" My response was that it was an act of faith. I was operating under God's promise that, when we lay hands on the sick, they will recover. I stepped out on His Word.

This is what we, God's flames of fire, must do. God is truth. He stands behind His Word and keeps the promises He made to us. We must trust in His promises to carry out the Great Commission and rest in His assurance that we will do even greater works than those done by Christ when He was on earth. We must trust the Holy Anointed One, Jesus Christ, beyond our faith and anointing of yester-year and yesterday. We must challenge Satan, defeat him in our lives, and be instruments of God to preach and teach others to defeat Satan in their lives.

Elijah went on Satan's turf only when God sent him and turned it into *God's captured hill* on Mt. Carmel. When we go into Enemy territory, we must be sure that God is our leader. Only when God leads us will we fight with faith, and with the knowledge and understanding of God and the Holy Spirit. God is our General in spiritual warfare. He knows where to lead us in strategic attacks against Satan. It is suicidal to go into the Enemy's territory without the leading and guidance of the Holy Spirit. We must reclaim the land and possessions that Satan has stolen from us, individually and collectively as the body of Jesus Christ. We must obey the leading of the Holy Spirit as God uses us.

Elijah knew, by faith in God, what he was doing on Mt. Carmel. We know, by faith in God, what we are doing. The absence of doubt comes from knowledge of God, Jesus Christ, and the working of the Holy Spirit. The absence of doubt comes from the heart's knowledge of God's Word. The absence of doubt comes from an intimate fellowship with God. This comes by fasting and prayer, obedience, praise, and worship. The absence of doubt comes through the presence of God's flaming fire in our hearts, through the diligent study of God's Word, and through faith in the promises of God, our consuming fire.

We must yield ourselves as vessels of God, channels through which He gets glory for Himself by manifesting His fire. God manifests His miraculous grace to soften man's heart and draw man to Him. Jesus knew this. Therefore, He performed many of

His miraculous works before men to confirm the Word of God that He preached and taught.

The nation of Israel had seen the power of God on many different occasions; yet, they intermittently slipped back into idol worship. On Mt. Carmel, God recalled the Israelite nation into worship with Him and away from the leadership of wicked kings like Ahab and those of Israel's past. Just as it was true in the past for Israel, it is true today. The world needs the holy men and women of God to humble themselves and pray, to hear from heaven, and to turn from every wicked way that prevents the power of God from bringing widespread revival. When we cry out, God will hear from heaven, forgive our sins, and heal the land. The wickedness in our nation and the world seems unprecedented; we need to look closer at biblical practices.

Drive-by shootings in some of our neighborhoods prevent people from sitting on their front porches. The government appears to support homosexuality. In Israel, the worship of idol gods included homosexual acts. Abortion is a controversial issue among the citizens and politicians in our nation. In Old Testament times, the people sacrificed babies to their idol gods. Today violence is at an all-time high in our schools and nation. Students, teachers, and administrators live in fear of violence on campus. Safety is an issue even with metal detectors at the schools' entrances and police patrolling the halls. We are an insecure people in an insecure nation that imprints "In God we trust" on our coins. Our behavior is not consistent with trust in God as a way of life.

The way back to safety and security is a return to God and a revival of faith in our hearts. We need pragmatic changes within our nation, from the highest government official to the lowest pauper. God wants to use His people, individuals called by His name, to work a miraculous spiritual change in all areas of our lives. He said: "If My people, which are called by my name, shall humble themselves, and pray, and seek my face, and turn from their wicked ways; then will I hear from heaven, and will forgive their sin, and will heal their land" (2 Chron. 7:14). God wants to heal our land of its social, economic, moral, and spiritual ills. He wants us to turn us into ministers, flaming fires to do just that.

Some situations and issues cause us to realize that we are between the proverbial rock and a hard place or between the Devil and the deep blue sea. Moses was at this hard place; Pharaoh and his army were behind Moses and the people he led, and the Red Sea was before them. Imagine, if you will, the 600 chosen chariots comprising the Egyptian king's army, the 50,000 horsemen, and the 200,000 footmen chasing a people not trained in warfare.

In the Exodus from Egypt, there were at least 5,000,000 Israelites on foot. To the natural eye they looked like a defenseless people. Yet, they trusted in the God who had miraculously delivered them from years of slavery. The God of their fathers Abraham, Isaac, and Jacob was their only defense and/or offense. His supernatural power was their refuge and fortress. He was their shelter in a weary land. God proved Himself as the One upon whom they could call, and *He was in the process of answering when they felt their cry to Him in their hearts before they verbally uttered their prayer.*

Moses, the man of God, knew this because he walked by faith according to the Spirit of God. Moses knew that God had not delivered them from Egypt to die in the desert. When God's flaming fires have such confidence in His deliverance, in His destruction of our enemies, and in His creation of a way where there appears to be no way, we too will walk boldly with faith in the God of our salvation. We, too, will see the God who knows us better than we know ourselves, the God who sees our victory before we experience it and desires to develop us into conquerors as He intervenes on our behalf. God said in Psalm 91:14–16: "Because he hath set his love upon me, therefore will I deliver him: I *will* set him on high, *because* he hath known my name. He shall call upon me, and *I will* answer him: I will be with him in trouble; I will deliver him, and honour him. With long life *will I* satisfy him, and shew him my salvation."

The God of heaven, our God, a Consuming Fire, delivered Moses and the Israelites using ten miraculous plagues. Moses, a type of Christ in the Old Testament, was God's channel, His vessel, if you will. Moses was the violin whose strings God plucked to produce the music that vibrated in Pharaoh's and the Egyptian peoples' ears until they were weary enough of this contentious strumming to set the people free. We, too, can be God's instruments who attack Satan and his demonic circumstances in our lives, and in the lives of the people to whom we minister, until Satan has no choice but to let God's people go to proclaim victoriously: "Free at last, free at last, thank God Almighty, we are free at last."

The Israelites, God's chosen people, experienced freedom in the wilderness after Pharaoh and his army attempted to capture them at the Red Sea. God's flame of fire, Moses, spoke to the people as Pharaoh approached: "Fear ye not, stand still, and see the salvation of the LORD, which he will shew to you to day; for the Egyptians whom ye have seen to day, ye shall see them again no more for ever. The LORD shall fight for you, and ye shall hold your peace" (Exod. 14:13–14). "And the angel of God, which went before the camp of Israel, removed and went behind them; and the pillar of the cloud went from before their face, and stood behind them: And it came between the camp of the Egyptians and the camp of Israel; and it was a cloud of darkness to them, but it gave light by night to these: so that one came not near the other all night" (Exod. 14:19–20).

Moses, God's man of the hour, set the stage for deliverance and freedom from the satanic powers that worked through Pharaoh.

> And Moses stretched out his hand over the sea; and the LORD caused the sea to go back by a strong east wind all that night, and made the sea dry land, and the waters were divided. And the children of Israel went into the midst of the sea upon dry ground: and the waters were a wall unto them

on their right hand, and on their left. And the Egyptians pursued, and went in after them to the midst of the sea, even all Pharaoh's horses, his chariots, and his horsemen. And it came to pass, that in the morning watch *the* LORD *looked* unto the host of Egyptians through the pillar of fire and of the cloud, and troubled the host of the Egyptians. And took off their chariot wheels, that they drave [sic] them heavily: so that the Egyptians said, "Let us flee from the face of Israel; for the LORD fighteth for them against the Egyptians." And *the* LORD *said* unto Moses, "Stretch out thine hand over the sea, that the waters may come again upon the Egyptians, upon their chariots, and upon their horsemen." And Moses stretched out his hand over the sea, and the sea returned to his strength when the morning appeared; and the Egyptians fled against it; and the LORD overthrew the Egyptians in the midst of the sea. And the waters returned, and covered the chariots, and the horsemen, and all the host of Pharaoh that came into the sea after them; there remaineth not so much as one of them. But the children of Israel walked upon dry land in the midst of the sea; and the waters were a wall unto them on their right hand, and on their left. Thus the LORD saved Israel that day out of the hand of the Egyptians; and Israel saw the Egyptians dead upon the sea shore. And Israel saw that great work which the LORD did upon the Egyptians: and the people feared the LORD, and believed the LORD, and his servant Moses.

—Exodus 14:21–31

It is important that we note the results of God's supreme power through Moses. Moses walked and *talked with God face to face*; God called him friend. Moses fellowshipped with Father God diligently and persistently; no matter what the circumstances, he was God's flaming fire who lived above the circumstances of life because of his faith in God who controls everything. This flaming fire of God, under the anointing of God, is not upon us just for ministry. The Holy Spirit is upon us for anointed living. We must live in fellowship with God and sensitivity to His Spirit as we walk in the boldness of the Holy Spirit. We must walk in the Spirit of God and not according to the deeds of the flesh. We must put the evil deeds of the body to death by living under the influence of the Spirit of God according to the dictates of God's Word in us.

The Spirit of God led Moses. When God told Moses, lift up thy rod, and stretch it over the sea and divide it, Moses knew, without a doubt that the voice was God's. He operated in God's Spirit. We must do likewise as God's flaming fires. Moses said to Israel, "Fear ye not, stand still, and see the salvation of the LORD, which he will shew you to day: for the Egyptians whom ye have seen to day, ye shall see them again no more for ever" (Exod. 14:13). Moses operated in complete faith that God would set his people free from the threat of death or slavery. If we are to be leaders used by God to set His people free, we must speak in faith calling those things that be not *as yet as though they already were.*

Moses did as God told him, and we must do the same. Moses' absolute obedience and yielding as God's channel resulted in the 1) hardening of the Egyptians' hearts, 2) honor (glory) from Pharaoh and his host, and 3) recognition in the Egyptians' hearts of the Great I AM, THE LORD.

As the Israelite nation observed God's destruction of Pharaoh and his armed forces in the Red Sea, they experienced the miraculous, supernatural anointing of God. Again, God showed His people that when Satan purposes a life or death situation in their lives, God saves, delivers, and keeps His people whole. They began to understand that a weapon formed against them would not prosper when God's anointed, the flaming fire minister, works on their behalf.

As I close this chapter, I cannot overlook Jesus, God's Anointed One. He is God's Ultimate and Greatest Flame of Fire. He is our model and example in lifestyle, in warfare, and in the use of His Holy Spirit's power. He is the Proficient User and Instrument through whom Father God works to teach us how to become flames of fire. It is, after all, about Him, not us.

CHAPTER 11

IT IS ABOUT CHRIST, NOT ABOUT US

For we are his workmanship, created in Christ Jesus unto good works, which God hath before ordained that we should walk in them.

—Ephesians 2:10

A young, attractive woman was talking to a friend who was quite interested in her. She mentioned to him that a former friend with whom she had been intimate was having a back problem. She inquired if her anointed minister friend would lay on hands for her injured friend. Without hesitation, he said, "Yes." With great surprise, she asked, "You would do that knowing he went with me?" The minister friend said, "Yes, it's about Him, not us."

This is a great principle for our lives: It is about Him, not us. This could have become an issue of selfishness, jealousy, and competition on the part of the anointed minister. He could have said to his inner man: "She's asking me to do something for a friend in whom she was more than interested. I'm not doing a thing for him. If she's still interested in him, this could ruin my chance of dating her. I'm real interested in her. He could be my competition." Out of love for God and his fellow man, however, he did not consider the possibility of competition. In the interest of Jesus' love for all men and the miraculous healing for a friend, he sought to bring glory to God.

How often have we seen selfishness, jealousy, and competition in God-called ministers who preach to their congregation against such weaknesses of the heart? How frequently can we observe one minister vying for position, power, and possessions in competition with a fellow minister of the same city, county, or state? This blight on the church of the living God is effective in preventing a real revival in our communities, state, and nation.

We overlook the division that accompanies competition. We forget that the house divided against itself cannot stand, and we continue to experience corruption and wickedness in the world. Vying for power and position in the church of the living God prevents the out-flowing, miraculously heavy glory of God from being in abundance in the lives of our church members. There is a vital need to recognize that, as brothers and sisters in the Lord, our greatest works and effectiveness lie in unity. The psalmist cried out for this in Psalm 133:1–3:

> Behold, how good and how pleasant it is for brethren to dwell together in unity! It is like the precious ointment upon the head, that ran down upon the beard, even Aaron's beard: that went down to the skirts of his garments; As the dew of Hermon, and as the dew that descended upon the mountains of Zion; for there the LORD commanded the blessing, even life for evermore.

God requires unity among His individual ministers and within the church. Division among our denominations must cease if the denominations are of God. (I am making an exception for any cult claiming to be a denomination.) Division among leaders must cease. We must put aside our individual and personal differences so that those of us in positions of authority can operate under the corporate anointing of the Lord. We must cease to be jealous of each other's achievements. We must stop envying the promotion of our brothers and sisters in the Lord and understand that our promotions come from the Lord. We must cease to compete for the largest or finest church. We must eliminate negative comparisons of church programs.

We must begin to edify each other and focus on saving souls and implementing the Great Commission. We are one body, although many members, in the Lord. Our baptism and infilling of the Holy Spirit are of the same God, the same Jesus Christ as Savior, the same Holy Spirit as Sealer of salvation and comfort.

Each minister's personality is different, and each church has its own personality. Each denomination may be different because of its doctrines and whether or not it operates with the same amount of knowledge of the Word of God and in the power of the anointing, yet we serve the same God with the same Holy Spirit. When Jesus died for Israel, He died for the gentiles also. When Jesus died for the gentiles, He also died for the future church. God does not expect us to be uniform; however, He is calling us to unify in Him. Ephesians 4:4–6 says, "There is one body, and one Spirit, even as ye are called in one hope of your calling; One Lord, one faith, one baptism, One God and Father of all, who is above all, and through all, and in you all."

Therefore, we are all under one anointing to be flames of fire, full of the fire of the Holy Spirit, with churches and ministries in or outside of the established churches. Moreover, our individual differences must be resolved in order for us to move in the flow of the Holy Spirit. God is moving with His Spirit upon the face of the earth to save us from destructive, moral decadence, including homosexuality, murder, drugs, prostitution, terrorism, rampant wickedness, and more.

The church of the living God must leave some things behind to be part of this movement of God's Spirit. Paul said, "Brethren, I count not myself to have apprehended: but *this one thing I do*, forgetting those things that are behind, and reaching forth unto those things which are before, I press toward the mark for the prize of the high calling of God in Christ Jesus" (Phil. 3:13–14).

We must never let our past rob us of our future as brothers and sisters in the Lord. As ministers, we must promote healing of the physical and emotional wounds in God's body, denominations, churches, and church organizations. Because we have grieved the Holy Spirit and held back the most effective work of Christ, let us refrain from this way toward one another as His corporate body:

> Let no corrupt communication (ill will) proceed out of your mouth, but that which is good to the use of edifying, that it minister grace to the hearers. And grieve not the holy Spirit of God, whereby ye are sealed unto the day of redemption. Let all bitterness, and wrath, and anger, and clamour, and evil speaking, be put away from you, with all malice: And be ye kind one to another, tenderhearted, forgiving one another, even as God for Christ's sake hath forgiven you.
> —Ephesians 4:29–32

When we apply these Scriptures to ourselves to eradicate jealousy, envy, competition, divisions, and differences, we shall catch on fire for God and our Jesus. We shall be endued with the power of the Holy Spirit as we have never known it before.

David said, "Behold, how good and how pleasant it is for brethren to dwell together in unity!" This is one of the few verses in the Word punctuated with the strong force and feeling of the exclamation point. This short sentence, one verse of Scripture, must be very important and central in God's scheme for us. So what is it like to dwell in unity?

Allow me to cite an experience with a group of anointed ministers of God who operated in the fivefold ministry or the offices of the church. I went to a North Carolina coastal town to establish a ministry. Feeling left out of the mainstream of the traditional churches, four full gospel churches formed an alliance. Even among these churches, however, some members changed their membership from one church to another. Hurt feelings resulted from these defections. Even though I was a new minister in the area, the executive board accepted me as a member. In discussion among the four churches, we developed procedures for accepting members from another church and encouraged unity and greater fellowship among all the churches.

The Spirit of God, with His anointing, became more powerful among us. Our fellowship and relationships became closer, more intimate and unified. The sisters and brothers of the different churches sensed this positive difference in the Lord. Therefore, they became friendlier. The spirit of the churches in attitude, manner of cooperating with each other, and love grew deeper in the Lord. We observed the love of Christ among us. The Holy Spirit of God wrought greater miracles among us all because we worked out our differences. It was good for us to dwell together in unity, and there was a definite difference in the ministers' wives. To our delight, they became sisters in the Lord.

What had happened? The corporate ointment of the brothers of our organization ran down on us even as the oil ran down from the head of Aaron onto his beard and went down to the skirts of his garments. As the dew of Mt. Hermon and the dew that descended upon the mountains of Zion was the same dew, even as the anointing upon you is the same anointing that is on me and was upon Christ; there was no need for comparison and competition. No need! Therefore, the Lord blessed our church ministries and us. The Holy Spirit unified us in service to the Lord. We experienced the greater heaviness of God's glory. This is one of the reasons that God created us—so that we could experience the heaviness of His anointing (glory) in the very midst of and on us.

God created us for Himself. He wanted to have a one-on-one relationship with our individual, unique personalities. In other words, even in God's creation, my personality is different from yours. Although Father God's principles for living and His purposes are the same for all of us, the way He deals with each of us is according to our uniqueness. For instance, you and I may listen to the same gospel message of God simultaneously, but what the message says to your situation and personality might be different from what is relevant to me. However, in Him, His purpose for creating us was so that you and I, in whatever field He has led us, might do good works. That's why Jesus said, "Let your light so shine before men, that they may see *your good works*, and *glorify* your father which is in heaven" (Matt. 5:16). God ordained us to do these good works. The Greek word for "ordain," *proetoimazo*, means "to prepare before." God prepared us and equipped us for good works and great exploits for Him before we were born. Jesus, the Anointed One, is the source of that preparation, that ordination. Having Him in us is all that we need, by His Holy Spirit, to be conformed to the image of Christ and to execute the gifts of the Spirit and fivefold ministry in the churches and this created world.

However, some of us hesitate to carry out the works of God under the anointing of the Holy Spirit because of fear of the Holy Spirit in our churches. This is the Devil's great power in God's church and in many denominations: fear of the Holy Spirit. We are okay in our preaching and teaching in God and other parts of the Word of God. We approve of the teaching on God and other parts of the Word of God. We approve of the teaching and preaching on Jesus, the Son of God and our Savior, but we are afraid of acknowledging and applying the doctrine of the Holy Spirit and operating under the anointing of God's Spirit. In seminary, some of our ministers are taught falsely that, when the apostles died, the gifts of the Spirit became inoperable in the church and the fivefold ministry was discontinued. We have accepted the Enemy's lie for too long. Satan knows that when the body of Christ awakes from its sleep to the great arsenal of weaponry in the Holy Spirit, his day is over or will soon end. We have been asleep far too long. We need a wake up call to the truth: *God has not changed.*

The principles and truths of Jesus that inspired the uneducated apostles of the early church to turn an upside down world of their day right side up are the same today. The same God of heaven and earth that worked through the early church with miraculous exploits in the Spirit is the same today. We need to let God be true and, if necessary, every man a liar. God says in Malachi 3:6, "For I am the LORD, I *change not*; therefore ye sons of Jacob are not consumed." God has not changed. The gifts of God in the Holy Spirit have not changed. Therefore, God wants His body of believers operating in the gifts of the Holy Spirit today. We should not be ignorant (lack knowledge) of these gifts of the Spirit in the church. The Bible states that God's people are destroyed for lack of knowledge. Paul said it well in 1 Corinthians 12:1–11:

> Now concerning *spiritual gifts*, brethren, *I would not have you ignorant. Ye know* that ye were Gentiles, carried away unto these dumb idols, even as ye were led. Wherefore I give you to understand, that *no man speaking by the Spirit* of God calleth Jesus accursed: and that no man can say Jesus is the Lord, *but by* the Holy Ghost. Now there are *diversities* of gifts, but the same Spirit. And there are differences of administrations, but the same Lord. And there are diversities of operations, but it is the same God which worketh all in all. But the manifestation of the Spirit is given to *every man* to profit withal. For to one is given by the Spirit the *word of wisdom*; to another the *word of knowledge* by the same Spirit; to *another faith* by the same Spirit; to another the *gifts of healing* by the same Spirit; To another the *working of miracles*; to another prophecy; to another *discerning of spirits*; to another *divers kinds of tongues*; to another the *interpretation of tongues*: But *all these* worketh that one and selfsame Spirit, dividing to *every man* severally as he will.

The traditional pastor and church have been afraid of these gifts of the Holy Spirit because they did not want to be criticized or ostracized, and some pastors, like me, have lost their churches. That is not important now; I lost my Baptist church because of the moving of God's Spirit in me. Before I share that experience with you, I would like to ask the pastors and my fellow Christians in traditional churches a few questions. Do we, in the full gospel or Pentecostal movement, not serve the same God that you claim to be your God and Spiritual Father? Is not Jesus the same Lord and Savior of all of us who know Him? Is not the Trinity—God, the Father, the Son, and His Holy Spirit, the same for you as He is for us? Of course, He is on all counts.

Therefore, what is there to be afraid of in the Holy Spirit? After all, did not Jesus say in Matthew 10:28, "And fear not them which kill the body, but are not able to kill the soul: but rather fear him which is able to destroy both soul and body in hell."

Let me speak to another area of fear about the traditional pastors and churches. This is not a criticism of the pastors or churches. That is not the purpose of this work. I have been where you are and done that, and do not want to do it again. The whole purpose of this work is to build up pastors and fellow Christians to realize and to inspire us, Christ's body, to activate and use the power of the Holy Spirit in us. We have suffered enough without His blessing us in this way. We have gone too long without the fire of the Holy Ghost in our midst. Real revival is delayed in our denominational churches. The Enemy, the Devil, has taken too many of our children, jobs, talents, gifts, marriages, families, books, careers, and prosperity. In summary, we have lost too much for too long because we fear allowing God's Holy Spirit to have His way in our lives and churches. Our fear of man has lasted too long, and every generation has suffered.

Because of our fears, homosexuals have been coming out of the closet since the late seventies, and to the extent that now they are financially and politically powerful, they influence the political leadership of our country. Indeed, we have homosexuals who are leaders in both secular and religious organizations.

Over the years, I asked myself this question: "When will God-called, God-sent, Spirit-filled ministers and pastors in our churches be courageous enough to come out of the closet, also? When will these pastors let their churches and the world know that they have been filled with and baptized in the Holy Spirit and that they will allow the Spirit of God to lead them?" When will my brothers of the cloth stop hiding the power of God and who they really are in the Lord?

I have come to several conclusions. First, pastors are afraid of losing their churches or having their salaries and benefits affected. These fears of material loss and criticism by fellow pastors have affected the leadership greatly. Secondly, the membership has unspoken beliefs that the church is devilish and cultish when they claim to operate in the gifts of the Spirit. Again, this reinforces the pastors' fears for they do not want to be labeled in their local church or in a county, district, state, or national organization.

Thirdly, the membership generally has too much financial power over the pastor. They hold the purse strings and many pastors, having made no investments on their own, are dependent on the income from the church. No pastor really wants his or his family's livelihood affected, and this instills understandable fear in his heart. Perhaps most importantly, many pastors lack faith in God and do not trust His promises. Nevertheless, God says in His word in Philippians 4:19, "But my God shall supply all your need according to his riches in glory by Christ Jesus." And if I may add, did not God say that the cattle upon a thousand hills are His? And the earth is the Lord's and the fullness thereof, the world and they that dwell therein . . . That we are not to take thought of what we shall eat, drink, or wear, for God clothes the plant life and feeds the fowl of air. Do we not know that He will provide for us?

The spirit of fear has gripped churches' leadership and followers. Paul said to timid Timothy, his son in the ministry in 2 Timothy 1:6–7, "Wherefore I put thee in remembrance that thou stir up the gift of God, which is in thee by the putting on of my hands. For God has not given us the spirit of fear; but *of power*, and *of love*, and *of a sound mind*."

Where there is fear, there is a lack of faith in God to provide for all of our needs—whatever they might be. Jesus will give us the courage, and the Holy Spirit will give His anointing power to teach and preach the full counsel of the Word of God including prosperity. There are so many verses in the Word that encourage us to walk in the things of God during the worst of times and with each new experience with God. I would just like to mention one or two things about your having the courage to take this bold step in the Lord. Note what it says in Isaiah 43:1–2:

> But now *thus saith* the LORD that created thee, O Jacob, and he that formed thee, O Israel, Fear not: for I have redeemed thee, I have called thee by thy name; thou art mine. When thou passest through the waters, I will be with thee; and through the rivers, they shall not overflow thee: when thou walkest through the fire, thou shalt not be burned; neither shall the flame kindle upon thee.

God's protection is with you, my fellow brothers and sisters. He protects us just as He said to Jacob and Israel that He would because He is the same today as He was then. God protects you as you walk by faith in Him and not according to sight.

The second Scripture for your edification is Isaiah 41:10: "Fear thou not; for I am with thee: be not dismayed; for I am thy God: I will strengthen thee; yea, I will help thee; yea, I will uphold thee with the right hand of my righteousness." It is right in the Lord that you take this step of faith. There are too many souls lost to the church and God's Kingdom because His people refused to step out on faith. Too many have gone to hell because we are not operating more powerfully in the gifts and the power of the anointing in the church.

Come out of the closet having been filled with the Holy Spirit. Come out of the closet with your baptism in the Holy Spirit. You know that you have spoken in tongues. You know that you have at least one gift of the Spirit. If you do not know, God will infill you with the power to exercise your unknown gift so that you may know it. Come out of the closet!

Let us get back to my experience in a traditional church. From the outset, I have never regretted the constructive change in my spiritual life and the new direction God gave me when I came out of the closet, filled with the Spirit and baptized in the Holy Spirit.

IT IS ABOUT CHRIST, NOT ABOUT US

Let me start at the beginning with my walk with Jesus. At nineteen years of age, I bowed on my knees in my mother's living room and asked the Lord to forgive me for my sins. Instantly, He saved me and in-filled me with His Holy Spirit. I shall never forget that He completely overshadowed me and baptized me with the Holy Ghost. I did not know it then, but I know it now. When Jesus came into my heart, in the person of the Holy Spirit, He placed the anointing of God's Holy Spirit in me. He is the Anointed One, our Messiah. He is Christos, the Anointed and the Anointing. I did not know the power of God within me to save, heal, and deliver people. No one around me in my church, neighborhood, or state seemed to know.

I know, however, that when I obeyed Him and honored my mother by addressing her as "Mother" rather than by her first name as she permitted us to do, he baptized me with the Holy Spirit again. I know that, when I was in fasting and prayer for souls that He baptized, He overshadowed me again with His Spirit. I do know that, within a year of accepting Jesus as my Savior, accepting God's call to enter the ministry, and praying, I was preaching to a congregation when ten persons in the service answered the call to accept Jesus as Lord and Savior. I understand that the *utmost purpose* of the *anointing* is to save the wicked, the corrupted, and the decadent in sin from the world's evil grip and Satan's kingdom even as God, for Christ's sake, saved me.

However, in spite of knowing that the church's purpose is to save souls, I was still perishing without the knowledge of the purpose of being filled and baptized in the Holy Spirit. God provided this wisdom as part of the purification process that I discussed in a previous chapter. During God's cleansing of me, He convicted and inspired me to start teaching the gifts of the Spirit, the doctrine of the power of attorney in Jesus' name. He led me to teach the congregation the full counsel of God from the Word of God. Having established my purpose, God led me to follow Him by faith.

In January of 1985, I started teaching the gifts of the Spirit at my pastorate. For two years, the teaching continued. It was effective; the Holy Spirit filled people, and miraculous healings occurred. God manifested Himself in all of His power and glory when He cast a demon out of a wheelchair-bound member and filled her with the Spirit of God. This member was living in a nursing home and had complained of pain continuously during the service. A professional nurse, who was also a church member, was beside her at the altar. The chairman of the deacon board was holding her wheelchair. Flowing with the Spirit, I said loudly: "Satan, leave God's child alone." Immediately she was overpowered in the Spirit. Her pains were gone. God gave her what she wanted in His power.

The demon left the sister, but Satan sent others of his soldiers to create confusion and chaos. Some members of the church accused me of teaching false doctrine. It was fine, it seems, for church members to be filled with the Holy Spirit and healed by the miraculous power of God, but casting out demons was going too far for those who were afraid of the Holy Spirit.

Unwittingly, I had committed political suicide. Members of the church whom I had never seen showed up and voted me out. On another occasion, the congregation voted me back in. Then a lawyer who said that he represented the church contacted me. During our meeting, he informed me that the church was willing to take out an injunction to bar me from the church grounds. The membership was afraid that the church would become full gospel like a well-known church in a nearby town. The lawyer said that the church was willing to offer me a sum of money if I did not return to the church.

Even though I learned later that the sum was $6,000, I did not accept it. I thought a church vote should settle the matter. After changing the church doors' locks, the deacon board took the matter into court. The court session convened after the church vote and verified that I was no longer the church's pastor.

Now allow me to clarify my position. I was not teaching and preaching in the fullness of the gospel of God for myself. It was about God and to benefit the church membership. My role was to be obedient to the leading of the Holy Spirit. Secondly, I did not accept the call of God nor enter the ministry for money. I am convinced in my belief that one should never compromise the gospel of Christ—not even for money. At that time, I preached three Sundays each month, and my annual salary was not $6,000. The deacon board chairman denied that the church authorized the lawyer to offer me money.

Even though I was paying a tremendous price for doing what God led me to do, I had to stand by my convictions. The power struggle was between *fear and faith*, *good and evil*, *God and Satan*, and between *my faith in God and selling out to Satan*. It was not about the church and me. Unfortunately, the majority of the church's membership was afraid of the Holy Spirit and of allowing God to have His way in the church, and the price of the anointing on me was not paid in full.

A fellow Baptist minister in the same community confronted me about operating in the Spirit. I looked directly into his eyes and told him, "Whatever I'm accused of, that's right. I do not deny it. I'm glad I am where I am with my faith in God." Astounded, he looked at me and jerked his head back in shock as if to say, he's owning up to being filled with the Spirit, laying on hands for healing, speaking and praying in tongues, and casting out demons. If these were his thoughts, he was right.

I have always believed that the truth can stand alone. I gladly confess that I am convinced that the Anointed One, Jesus Christ, wants every church—regardless of denomination—filled and baptized in the Holy Spirit. He wants His God-called, God-sent ministers filled and baptized with the Holy Spirit. He also wants you and me, fellow laborers in the gospel, to be ministers—flames of fire who preach and teach with the power and fire of the Holy Spirit so intense that it will burn sin and its consequences out of the lives of men.

The Holy Spirit burned the sin of adultery out of my life when I asked God to forgive me. He can burn drug and alcohol addiction, prostitution, homosexuality, stealing, murder, adultery, and any other wickedness or sin out of a person's life. That is the intensity of the fire of God and power within us, my fellow ministers and Christians.

God blessed me to operate under the Anointed One with His power while He brought glory to Himself in laying on of hands for healing. I have seen sight restored to people, hearts healed of a massive heart attack, and demons cast out. I have seen people overshadowed in the Spirit just by directing my hand toward them, and people were overpowered in the Spirit just by speaking the Word of prophecy to them. My preaching and teaching have been filled with the fire of the Spirit. I sent the Word of healing to Argentina, South America, and a hospitalized lady was healed of cancer. The Word has changed lives and sent individuals and churches in God's direction because of the word of prophecy spoken through me. I have been a participant in the miracles of the Holy Ghost. Today, my strongest desire is to save souls, and my goal is to heal men and women of sickness and disease. Without God's saving grace through the faith and power of the Spirit, everyone is lost, and they must be saved. This is God's ultimate purpose for us.

We must preach and teach with the burning incinerator of the Spirit so that God can bring revival to our churches, communities, cities, states, and nation and to the world. The world is corrupt and corrupting, and unless the churches of the Living God yield to God's purpose and His will to stop it, we will self-destruct in sin. God wants to use us His leaders as instruments of His power and glory to restore and reconcile the worlds' peoples unto Him. God called us to work in His vineyards to save the lost and equip them with His Word. Our task is great, but God will do it if we purpose to do His will on earth as His flames of fire. It is all to His glory, not ours. We are just the recipients of His blessings after doing His good will.

God has brought me back in this writing to the area of fear. He revealed to me that there is a certain amount of selfishness in fear. Fear keeps God's ministers from doing His will. We question our security and our sanity: "What happens to me if I yield to God's Spirit of infilling and baptism? What happens if I speak in tongues in the language of the Spirit? What happens to me if I lay on my hands for healing, casting out demons, teaching and preaching the full counsel of the Word of God? What happens to me as a pastor and leader of God among my church members, peers, and colleagues? What happens to me on the local, state, and national level? If I operate in the Spirit, what will people say about me?"

Please observe the selfishness of these questions: "What happens to *me*?" The emphasis, taken off God, is now on the individual. This is the selfishness of fear. God requires His servants to replace fear with faith, and He provides the power to endure whatever man might say or do. In Isaiah 54:17, God promises, "No weapon that is formed against thee shall prosper; and every tongue that shall rise up against thee in judgment thou shalt condemn. This is the heritage of the servants of the LORD, and their righteousness is of me, saith the LORD." It works, my fellow Christians. The weapon may be formed, but God will not allow it to prosper, to hurt you beyond your endurance. We condemn the opposing tongues as we speak against them. This is our heritage in the Lord.

It is past time for us to come out against the instruments of Satan, people who judge us inappropriately or falsely, with the power of God's Word in speaking condemnation to the tongues. After all, our warfare is against the echelons of Satan, of principalities and powers, spiritual wickedness in high places, and the rulers of darkness. Our warfare is not against flesh and blood; it is against the evil motivating forces behind man's actions. We must recall Romans 8:31: "What shall we then say to these things? If God be for us, who can be against us?"

If you are anxious or worried, God has a word for you: "For promotion cometh neither from the east, nor from the west, nor from the south. But God is the judge: He putteth down one, and setteth up another" (Ps. 75:6–7). We can conclude, then, the Lord is the source of our promotions. Seriously, would you rather that God or man be mad with you? I would chose man, for when a man's ways please God, He makes his enemies to be at peace with him. Selfish fear out, the love of God and fellow man in. Selfish fear out, saved souls in. Selfish fear out, the will of God in to God's glory, not ours.

God miraculously works through you, when you yield to His Spirit and become a flame of fire for Him. He will absolutely blow your mind as to who you are in Him and the magnificent, boundless measure of His power within you. None of us knows who we really are in Him until we begin to realize what He is developing us to be. This is an ongoing work of God.

Years ago, had someone told me, "George, God has a book for you to write to His called ministers and to the body of Christ," I would have looked puzzled and not believed it. Yet I am finishing this work. The developing power of the will of God manifests to us that the real you does not show up until He develops your potential in Him.

When this happens, we should not become proud or arrogant for it is the power of the Anointed One and His anointing works in us according to the uniqueness of our personality. I can tell you from experience: Tempting thoughts will come to you to make you feel proud and pompous and to take credit for the spiritual works that God does through you. Remember: It is about Him, not us. Resist the thoughts, and the Devil will flee from you. Men, women, and youth will shower you with accolades. Yet, you must remember this: It is about Him, Jesus Christ, not you. When this principle is instilled in our spirits, we are firmly established and secure in God, and the forces of evil cannot move us.

God said to Isaiah:

> Thus saith God the LORD, he that created the heavens, and stretched them out; he that spread forth the earth, and that which cometh out of it; he that giveth breath unto the people upon it, and spirit to them that walk therein: "I the LORD have called thee in righteousness, and will hold thine hand, and will keep thee, and give thee for a covenant for the people, for a light of the Gentiles; to open the blind eyes, to bring out the prisoners from the prison, and them that sit in darkness out of the prison house. I am the LORD: that is my name: and my glory will I not give to another, neither my praise to any graven images."
>
> —Isaiah 42:5–8

It is about Him, not us! It is about His work through the ages, His works in the present, His works in and through the heart of man. He will not give us His glory or praise, but He *will share* His heavy anointing with us to do mighty exploits for Him. It is about Him, never about us! Praise God, Praise God, alleluia to the King of kings, the Lord of lords, to Him who sits upon His throne looking low on us, the children of men. *To God be the Glory, for the great things He has done.*